Coaching the Crosswind

Practical answers to the questions coaches ask

JANE HARDERS

Coaching the Crosswind
ISBN 978-1-915483-54-6

Published in 2024 by Right Book Press
Printed in the UK

© Jane Harders 2024

The right of Jane Harders to be identified as the author of this work has been asserted in accordance with the Copyright, Designs and Patents Act 1988.

A CIP record of this book is available from the British Library.

All rights reserved. No part of this book may be reproduced, stored in a retrieval system, or transmitted in any form or by any means, electronic, mechanical, photocopying, recording or otherwise, without the prior written permission of the copyright holder

Illustrations, layout and cover design by Natalie Scott, who interpreted the author's concepts so perfectly.

Coaching is a contact sport

Our instincts are honed **on the field** – during conversations with clients and in our reflections afterwards.

There are no shortcuts. Just **practice**.

INTRODUCTION
Welcome to *Coaching the Crosswind*

This book is inspired by the many coaches that I've worked with over the last 20-plus years, and the questions they've asked me as their peer, tutor or supervisor.

From our conversations, I've noticed a recurring pattern in the questions coaches ask – whether they're a developing coach (still studying for a qualification), newly qualified (and now developing in the real world) or are an experienced coach with thousands of hours of practice under their belt.

Wherever you are in your coaching journey you're likely to have some of these same questions.

I don't claim to have all the answers – in fact, I'd argue that a coach who believes that they're fully formed or fully skilled is invariably lacking in self-awareness – but I've taken the most common "How do I...?" questions and answered them with a range of tried-and-tested tips, tools and strategies.

I'm a practising coach (or should that be "coach-in-practice"?) and I split my time 50/50 between my own client coaching work and the development of other coaches through training and supervision.

"Coaching the crosswind" takes a practice-based – rather than an academic – approach.

Through my own laboratory of coaching hours – and the coaching hours of my students and supervisees – we've tried and tested these approaches and techniques; we know that they work in real-life coaching assignments and conversations.

This book is NOT intended to replace the inputs and insights that you get from a supervision relationship. Instead, think of it as a first point of reference or a "go-to" guide for effectively handling those inevitable "sticky" moments, common questions and dilemmas that all coaches encounter.

Practical answers to the questions coaches ask.

I hope you'll enjoy exploring Crosswind and that some of your most frequently asked questions are answered here.

Language and terminology

Coachee = client

You might notice that I prefer to use the word "client" instead of "coachee; it's a matter of personal preference and I feel that the double "ee" implies a certain passivity – someone who is "done to" rather than a fully engaged partner that you're journeying alongside.

If you're coaching within an organisation (where your coachees are also your colleagues), the word "client" might sound out of place. But I'm deliberately using it throughout this book; I feel that "client" conveys working together in line with their agenda. They're in control of the focus and content of your time together – and the actions which follow.

Other authors use alternative descriptors such as "player" (Myles Downey) or "thinker" (Nancy Kline). I'm going to stick with "client" but please feel free to substitute your own favourite term as you read. It's your exploration.

> **Coachee/client/player/thinker**
> **=**
> **The other person in your coaching partnership**

Process = assignment

The word "process" is often used when referring to the coaching journey – either at the macro level (from coach selection to closing) or micro level (within an individual coaching conversation). Talking about coaching as a process can make it sound cold, linear and unforgiving – not at all like the partnerships we create when working with a coaching client. Instead, I'll refer to coaching "assignments" and the best-practice stages within both the micro level of the conversation and the macro end-to-end journey.

> **Process = assignment**
> **Macro = end-to-end assignment**
> **Micro = within the coaching conversation**

How the book is structured

The two parts of the book separate the micro – which is everything you'll encounter in your coaching conversations – from the macro, which is all about managing the wider assignment.

In Part 1 you'll find practical, tried-and-tested techniques that you can use in every day coaching conversations.

Part 2 looks in detail at the key stages of a formal coaching assignment and gives frameworks, suggested content and examples to help you facilitate these crucial conversations with fluency and confidence.

Each chapter tackles specific "How do I...?" or "What should I...?" questions.

At the end of each chapter you'll find a one-pager "At a glance" summary of answers to the question posed throughout the chapter.

Finally, at the end of the book there's a quick-reference guide to the tools covered.

Why "Coaching the Crosswind"?

Many complex challenges can be simplified by using imagery or metaphors – and they provide a rich seam of exploration when offered by our coaching clients.

The "Coaching the crosswind" concept came to me after a walk on the beach near my house; I'd been trying to walk north along the shoreline, and a strong easterly wind kept pushing me across the beach towards the cliffs. I made little (if any) progress – until I decided to work with the force of the wind instead of battling against it. The wind blew me along (and up) the beach until I reached the cliffs. In the lee of the cliffs the force of the wind was lessened and I could walk northwards with relative ease.

The following day I was in a supervision conversation where a coach was telling me about her efforts to keep a client on track. Her client kept wanting to divert to an alternative agenda. My battle on the beach and the need to go with the wind – not against it – popped into my mind. And so the metaphor of "coaching the crosswind" was born. See Chapter 4.

For developing coaches, rich metaphors or vivid imagery can help anchor an idea or concept. I hope the metaphors I have come up with for this book will resonate and create new insights for you. For those of you who prefer lived examples, I've included a sprinkling of mini case studies and stories from supervision conversations.

And finally...

My grateful thanks to the coaches and coach-students whose questions have inspired me to explore, test and shape my thinking. As coaches, we recognise the power of asking questions and the insights that can emerge.

Thank you for the gift of your questions.

Contents

PART 1: UNDER THE MICROSCOPE
THE COACHING CONVERSATION   9

CHAPTER 1: **HANGING ON A THREAD…**   11
❝ What if I can't think of a question?

CHAPTER 2: **SERVING SOGGY QUICHE**   25
❝ How can I avoid going round in circles in a coaching conversation?

CHAPTER 3: **SLIPPING OUT OF "ASK" GEAR**   33
❝ How can I avoid giving advice when I'm supposed to be coaching?

CHAPTER 4: **COACHING THE CROSSWIND**   47
❝ When a client goes off-topic, how can I get them back on track?

CHAPTER 5: **PACE AND FLOW – QUICKSTEP OR WALTZ?**   55
❝ How do I speed up/slow down/change direction/get a word in?

CHAPTER 6: **WHAT IFS – A PICK AND MIX**   63

PART 2: THE BIG PICTURE
MANAGING THE RELATIONSHIP, MANAGING THE ASSIGNMENT   71

CHAPTER 7: **CHEMISTRY – SAMPLING THE FLAVOURS**
❝ How do I run a chemistry meeting?

CHAPTER 8: **CONTRACTING – THE JOURNEY BEGINS**   89
❝ What do I need to cover in a contracting meeting?

CHAPTER 9: **MAINTAINING COURSE AND MOMENTUM**   107
❝ The assignment is losing momentum… what can I do?

CHAPTER 10: **CLOSING – JOURNEY'S END**   119
❝ What do I need to cover in the final session?

PART 3: RESOURCES AND REFERENCES
USEFUL STUFF   131

Section 1: Tools and where to find them

Section 2: More about – additional Chapter-related resources

Section 3: References

Coaching is just a conversation

Deceptively simple, nuanced and complex.

Where thinking happens out loud.

PART 1: UNDER THE MICROSCOPE
The coaching conversation

In this part of the book we'll explore some of the most frequently asked questions – the kind of questions that are on a coach's mind immediately after a coaching conversation. The everyday questions that we ask ourselves (or anxiously fret over) when we're reflecting on the conversation and how we feel it went.

> **What could I – what SHOULD I – have done when…?**
> **How could I have handled…?**

All of the questions relate directly to the micro elements of our coaching – within the actual conversations with our clients – and so the visibility of any technical challenges we encountered are limited to us, and our client.

Just because you felt that your questioning was clunky or you'd have liked to pin something down more specifically DOESN'T mean that the client didn't derive enormous value from it. The technical stuff is your agenda, not theirs.

The quality of the conversation should be viewed through the client's eyes.

Having focused time to explore your thoughts and be listened to – without judgement or opinion – is rarer than hen's teeth. So giving your clients a "damn good listening to" – in a safe, non-judgmental space – is worth its weight in gold.

Being present is infinitely more important than technical perfection. And afterwards – when we're writing our reflections/journal – that's when we can self-challenge, critique our approach, examine what worked (or didn't work) and find new learning.

> **Leave your technical critic at the door; it's unhelpful and distracting.**
> Giving full-beam attention means 100% focus on your client.
> Bringing our technical reflections into a session steals the agenda.

In the following chapters we'll unpick some of the common challenges that sit within a coaching conversation, share a range of tried-and-tested techniques and hopefully answer some of your niggling "How do I…?" and "What could I…?" questions.

All of the content is practice-based and – if you recognise some of the metaphors or stories from supervision or conversation – then you might just have been my inspiration for the chapter.

Great questions

The skill of questioning is the **ability to create great questions in the moment**.

Questions which are **tailored to fit the need and context of this specific conversation**.

Questions which **invite and inspire provoke and challenge, expand and enable**.

CHAPTER 1
Hanging on a thread...

Possibly the greatest fear expressed by many coaches is the prospect of not being able to come up with a question in the moment. It's been described to me in the following ways:

- "My mind went blank. I was frantically trying to think of a question – I panicked."
- "I felt the conversation was hanging in mid-air; I literally didn't know what to ask next."

So in this chapter we'll look at:

What if I can't think of a question?

You've been asking questions since you first learned to speak – starting with childish repetitions of "why", and then applying that curiosity to conversations. So the practice of asking questions is already embedded in your conversational style.

You already hold a "Questioning Proficiency" badge. So you can be pretty confident that you'll find a question to ask.

"What did you have for breakfast today?"

"Where did you go on your last vacation?"

It just might not be a great question – or particularly relevant/useful in this conversation.

So let's have a quick run through of some core principles around questioning:

Principle #1: How to ask a great coaching question: Make it...
- **Contextual** – relevant to the issue/context/challenge/landscape
- **Connected** to the immediate conversation/previous responses
- **Contribute** to the client's exploration

Every question needs to earn its place and have a purpose. So be clear about what you're trying to achieve by asking the question.

Principle #2: Purpose: What are you trying to achieve by asking it?
- **Understand** the issue/context/challenge/landscape?
- **Clarify** or confirm?
- **Dig deeper?** Find out a greater level of detail/feeling/history.
- **Go wider?** Expand the client's thinking or perspectives.

Now – let's address this notion of finding the "right" question in a coaching context.

> **Principle #3: The "right" question: There's not just one.**
> In any given situation there could be hundreds of questions that would be effective – and dozens which could be classed as "great". Your responsibility is to create a question that is effective in THIS conversation, at THIS moment in time.

In trying to find, refine and distil options internally for the "perfect" question – or mentally running through lists of learned questions – you're disconnecting from the conversation; you've stopped listening. And you're not fully present in the conversation.

- "The fear of not finding a question became my focus; my mind was desperately racing."

It's this internal dialogue – and its impact on your listening and presence – which will stunt your ability to craft a question. Your logical brain can't function when your emotional one takes over. You need to be listening and present to create effective questions.

> **Principle #4: What makes a question "powerful"?**
> A powerful question will make a person stop and think. They'll go quiet.
> It's the combination of context, relevance and timing – what's "powerful" for one person may have zero impact on another. Powerful questions can't be found on a standard list.

You might have developed some go-to starter questions for different situations – but we cannot pre-prepare a list of questions, or learn them by rote. No list is going to serve every context or situation and your client will spot standard off-the-shelf questions.

Powerful questions are bespoke and tailored to the client and the conversation.

And – in any case – however long your list is, you can't stop the conversation in mid-flow whilst you consult your Fabulous Book of Super-Useful Questions.

> **Principle #5: Silence is okay. It's not a race to respond.**
> You don't need to fill it – or reframe the question. Or ask another.
> If you've asked a question which resonates, the client may go quiet. Respect the silence; give them space and time to think.

Silence provides thinking time for both parties; it's not a judgement on your skill and ability. If you've asked a question that's meaningful or challenging to the client, let it sit. Good conversation has a pace that's varied – it's not a race to respond. (See Chapter 5 for tips on pacing.) And if you need time to think, signpost the pause. See question type #8, Pause questions.

Stop and check: Where am I in my exploration?

This is about navigating within the conversation. Are you trying to:

- **stay on the same thread** and **explore further around the current topic** by going deeper or wider? or
- **move onto a different thread/topic** – or another stage of the conversation?

Recognising where you are/where you want to focus the questions helps to identify the various types of questions you might want to use, and signposts your logical brain – in a moment of panic – to the relevant box of tools and techniques.

Threads and nuggets

Let me just explain my references to the concept of threads; when we review a coaching conversation we'll notice that there were various threads to the conversation. Different themes that we explore through questioning.

I always think of these threads as vertical – we start at the top with an initial question, and then drill down and explore via a series of linked questions.

> **Visualise – An evening performance at Cirque du Soleil.**
> Like an aerial performer, the coach deftly and skilfully works down the rope (thread), as the client's responses sway the rope from side to side, informing and shaping the next question.

Each thread might have several strands to it – some will be longer, more complex and create more insights for the client than others.

Others may be simple, short and taut.

We may revisit and pull some threads more than once – noticing where and how that thread connects with others. And how some threads are stronger, offer more resistance or challenge than others.

The threads may overlap, pull against each other – but all of the threads together form the rich tapestry of the client's world.

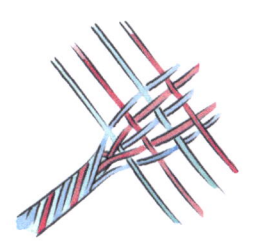

So, what determines where a thread will start and what we'll explore?

Nuggets – panning for gold

What's a nugget – and how do we spot them?

In any conversation, our questioning focuses around content provided to us by the client – we might get general topics (their role/ambitions/challenges etc) or the areas we choose to explore may be highlighted through their language. e.g. emotive words, repetition of specific words, or words which appear incongruous or at odds with other things they're saying.

These are the nuggets – the above-the-ground indications of something to be further explored. Whether or not they lead to a rich seam of discovery is ours to find.

Quick Tip-in-Practice: When spotting nuggets listen for:
- **Emotive words**
- **Patterns or repetitions** of the same word
- **Omissions** – what's NOT said or left out
- **Anomalies** – discrepancies or contradictions

Listening for nuggets is a key skill for coaches; we listen, we notice and we mentally "park" it to go back to and pick up later. These nuggets provide us with a bank of key themes (threads) to explore within a coaching conversation.

Using QAQA: Question-Answer-Question-Answer

Typically we'll explore "nuggets" through the use of linked questioning – QAQA – where the previous answer informs the next question.

Also known as "linear probing", QAQA simply means that the answer to your first question becomes the "parent" of your next question. And so on.

Here's a quick example of using responses to create the next question.

> *Coach*: How is the project going?
>
> *Client*: It's been really **challenging**.
>
> *Coach*: In what way **challenging**?
>
> *Client*: It's been **hard** getting hold of the key **resources**.
>
> *Coach*: What makes it **hard**/what specific **resources** are **hard** to get?

Hanging a question off a previous answer demonstrates great listening – and provides a solid "feed" of questions. Plus, it's linear – so you can easily visualise travelling down a thread.

Once that thread is exhausted, you choose another of your parked nuggets to explore. And begin a new thread of questions.

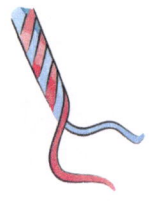

Back to the exploration: If you're trying to:

Move on to explore another thread (or stage of the conversation)

If you feel that the current topic/thread has been fully explored, and there are no additional angles or perspectives, then it's time to move on to another thread.

To move smoothly from one thread to another, use summary, then a playback intro (see below) followed by a question relating to the new nugget.

> **Quick Tip-in-Practice: Use summary to move from one thread to another.**
> - **Summarise** – We've talked about a,b,c,d and e...
> - **Playback**: You mentioned x earlier...
> - **Question**: ... tell me more about that.

This helps the transition from one topic to another appear seamless. Playing back a summary of what's been explored in one thread helps to "close off" that thread – and gives you a few seconds to choose your next nugget and frame your question. (Summary also works brilliantly to transition smoothly from one stage of the session framework to another. See Chapter 2: "Soggy quiche".)

You'll notice that – in the Quick Tip above – we used a playback intro followed by a question; I refer to this as a "wrapped" question.

Wrapped vs standalone questions

Regardless of the type of question asked (more on question types shortly), in my view there are essentially only two basic constructions for a question:

1. Wrapped – where a short element of playback precedes the question, e.g.

"You mentioned x; tell me more about that."

"You've used the phrase "utterly ridiculous" four times; what makes the situation "utterly ridiculous"?

2. Standalone – as it says on the tin. A question which has no "wrapping" (my word for preceding playback or positioning).

"Tell me more about x."

"What makes the situation "utterly ridiculous"?

A good flow of questions contains both wrapped and standalone questions; mix it up to ensure there's sufficient agility in your questioning. Wrapped questions enable us to link content, to circle back to earlier themes – and pick up new threads.

Wrapped questions contain verbal signposting – if overused, the client anticipates where you're going to go and it becomes repetitive for the client – potentially impacting on the level of engagement and challenge.

Christine's story: Climbing the North face of the Eiger

Christine is a coach-in-training. After circa 30 hours of practice coaching, she was despondent and declared to me "I can't do this. My questioning is really clumsy – I can't find the questions in time to ask them fluently. I'll never make a good coach if I can't ask questions. And I'm exhausted at the end."

I asked Christine to make a video recording of a coaching session (with the client's permission) for supervision purposes.

I watched the recording and it was instantly apparent that Christine was climbing the North face of the Eiger – she was taking the hardest possible route with her questioning. She'd chosen the black route.

Every question was a standalone question; for an entire hour she had constructed standalone questions without a shred of playback. She was climbing a sheer cliff face. No time to think or plan – or rest on a ledge; just a relentless Question-Answer-Question-Answer rally, in which Christine had "played" over 30 questions.

When I pointed this out to Christine her relief was palpable. She re-watched the video through a "wrapped" vs "standalone" lens and could see how hard she'd made it for herself by using 100% standalone questions. She recognised that the "crafting" of each standalone question had drained her, and – at times – taken her attention away from the client to focus on creating her next question. At times she had stopped listening.

Having had her lightbulb moment, she set out to incorporate more wrapped questions into her next coaching session. We met three months later and she was grinning from ear to ear as she spoke:

"I CAN do this. Incorporating some wrapped questions helps my client hear their words back – and gives me time to plan a better question off the back of it.

And I'll never take the black route again."

In this example the coach used 100% standalone questions; as well as making it harder for herself, her client was denied the opportunity to hear their own words played back.

Using 100% wrapped questions also has drawbacks – primarily that the signposting of topics through playback can become repetitive and enables the client to anticipate where you're going next. You need to retain the element of surprise, so mix it up.

Quick Tip-in-Practice: Mix it up.
Use a combination of wrapped and standalone questions.
Playback followed by a command/TED question (Tell, Explain, Describe) is a simple recipe.
Vary the playbacks: You said earlier.../You mentioned.../I heard...
Vary the questions: Tell me.../What makes...?/How does...?/Describe...

Back to the exploration: If you're trying to:

Stay on the same thread and explore the current topic further

The art of questioning is the ability to create great questions – in the moment – which are relevant to the **context; connect** to the previous answers; and **contribute** to the client's active exploration.

As we said earlier, be clear about what you're trying to achieve with your question:

> - Understand the issue/context/challenge/landscape?
> - Clarify or confirm?
> - Dig deeper? Find out a greater level of detail/feeling/history.
> - Go wider? Expand the client's thinking or connect across other threads.

Once you've identified your purpose, it's simply about applying a range of question types to create your question.

Question types – a summary

#1 Open and closed questions: We're all familiar with the concept of open and closed questions. They're the bedrock of everyday conversation.

- **Open questions:** Used to open up conversation and explore the context of an issue or challenge, open questions deliberately seek longer answers and invite an expansive response. We aim to ask more open than closed questions.
- Broad in context, open questions start with: What /How/Who/When – and Why.
  - **Why not why?** Whilst why forms the basis for an open question, it can cause the recipient to become defensive, or try to justify their position – or even shut down. Be aware of it within your coaching "palette" – use it deliberately. There are better options, i.e. "What makes you say…?"
  - What and how are used (on average) 3x more than when, where and who.
- **Closed questions:** Narrow in focus, usually answered with a single word or choice from multiple-choice answers, and can be used to confirm, clarify or close down options. Often begin with: Are/Is/Can/Could/Would… you or it. E.g. Would you/Could you/Can you/Is it/Would it.

> **Quick Tip-in-Practice: Listen to the first three words of your questions to identify your current patterns. (Listen to a recording or ask an observer.)**
> - How often did you start with "Can you…" or "Could you…" Even if this invitation was followed by an open question, it can close the client down.
> - How often did you ask "where", "when" or "who" questions? And why?

#2 TED questions: Really useful alternatives to preface an open question, TED questions (also known as command questions) are short for "Tell, Explain, Describe". These questions provide a variation by dialling up the strength of the invitation.

From invitation to "command", TED can be applied to both question and statement forms.

"**Tell me**... what does that look like?" – *question form*

... what that looks like." – *invitational statement form*

"**Explain**... what do you mean by x?" – *question form*

... what you mean by x." – *invitational statement form*

The third command is used purely as a statement/command:

"**Describe**... what x looks like."

Quick Tip-in-Practice: Use TED questions specifically and sparingly.
TED works well within a wrapped question, following a playback:
e.g. You mentioned x; tell me more about that.
Vary the TED questions and don't use them in consecutive questions; too many repetitive command questions can impact tone/rapport.

These first two types of questions are broad questioning tools, useful for general exploration around an issue or topic, and to help gain a fuller understanding of the landscape.

The third question type is used to find out more information, at the next level down.

#3 Precision questions: Are used to drill down – they're really useful when we want to get to that second layer of information, to dig deeper into something that's already been said, to travel further down into the thread of questioning.

Precision questions contain precision words:

Specifically – Precisely – Exactly – In detail

Quick Tip-in-Practice: Specifically – Precisely – Exactly – In detail.
Precision words can be used as wrapped or standalone questions.
Specifically, what are you aiming to achieve with xyz?
You mentioned xyz; what specifically are you aiming to achieve?

The simple inclusion of a precision word digs out more detail than a standard open/general question and often elicits more nuggets.

#4 Expansion questions: Really simple, really useful questions when you want to go wider/expand the client's response. Expansion questions are designed to invite further inputs from the client after an initial response.

Typically made up of "What else"/"Anything else"/"And what else" phrases.

> **Quick Tip-in-Practice: What else/Anything else/And what else?**
> Can be combined with summary to form a wrapped question:
> *You've mentioned working on a,b,c and d; what else have you worked on?*
> Or as a simple standalone invitation question after a client input:
> *"Anything else?"*

#5 Missing questions: Similar to expansion questions, but in reverse. A missing question plays back a summary of the client's responses to date, and invites them to spot what's missing/fill the gap in their description and expand on their original input.

> **Quick Tip-in-Practice: What haven't you mentioned/covered yet?**
> Can be combined with summary to form a wrapped question:
> *You've mentioned a,b,c and d; what haven't you talked about yet?*
> Interestingly, 9 out of 10 clients will add something else when invited!

#6 Flip or reverse questions: This is a technique designed to help the client when they're stuck – particularly useful when trying to identify goals or strategies. If your client is struggling to come up with a response that's framed forward/in a positive way, flip it to identify the opposite – past experience/a negative. Or vice versa.

When the human brain can't envisage something, it creates perceived barriers or a "don't know" response; a flip or reverse question leverages the mental barrier to create an alternative "flipped" perspective. Let the weight of the original question flip it over.

> **Quick Tip-in-Practice: Use reverse AFTER asking the original question.**
> Q: What would you like to project as your personal brand?
> A: Don't really know.
> Q: *What do you NOT want to project?*
> **Ask the flip question only AFTER you've tried the first version.**

Literally hundreds (possibly thousands?) of variations can be applied:

"What do you most want (least want)... to happen/to achieve...?"

"Tell me what constitutes a "good" ("bad")... result/outcome.

"Where are you most (least)... confident/experienced/skilled?

"What enables (disables)...?"

#7 Agile questions – You'll NEVER be without a question

This model is – quite simply – your passport to always having a relevant question.

I came across the "4 Cornerstones" model in Peter Hill's *Concepts of Coaching* (Hill 2004) many years ago, and have adapted it into an Agile version. The beauty of this approach is that you can create a new perspective or new thread of thinking at any given moment in time.

Questions direct the exploration in one of four directions. You can use one direction – or more (which is useful if you're shaking down/testing out ideas or strategies) – and the questions are almost content free. They're not dependent on previous answers and this makes them super-useful as standalone questions.

The four categories explore and direct the client's thinking in four different directions: up/down/forward/back

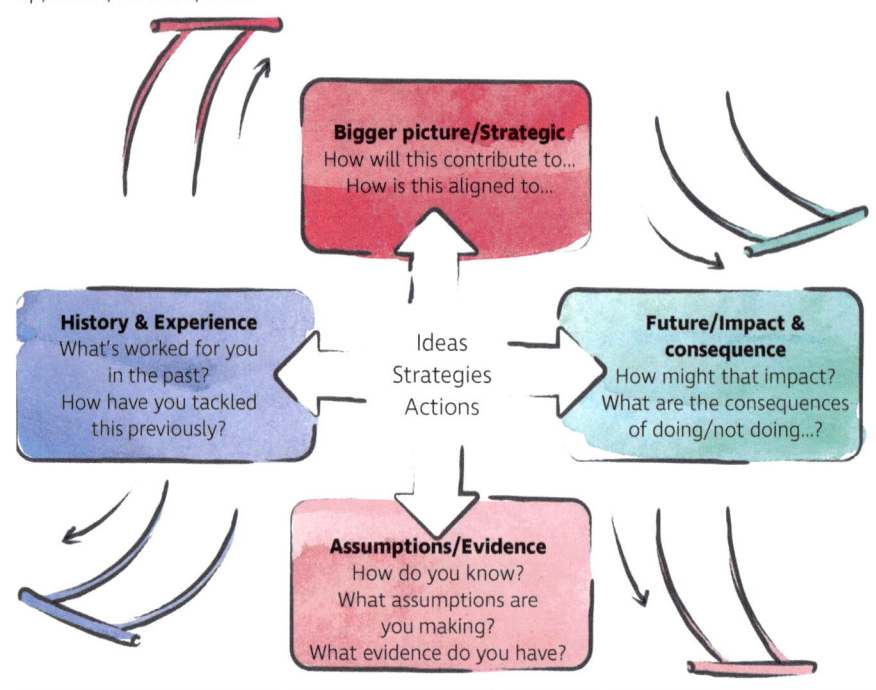

Bigger picture/Strategic
How will this contribute to...
How is this aligned to...

History & Experience
What's worked for you in the past?
How have you tackled this previously?

Ideas
Strategies
Actions

Future/Impact & consequence
How might that impact?
What are the consequences of doing/not doing...?

Assumptions/Evidence
How do you know?
What assumptions are you making?
What evidence do you have?

There are always four trapezes within reach that you can swing onto

More sample questions can be found in Part 3. We all have a natural preference for some directions over others, and will use them more frequently. Track your pattern and try out asking questions from your current least-used directions.

Quick Tip-in-Practice: Experiment with different directions.
Down questions are brilliant to test generalisations and assumptions. Combine different directions in questioning threads *e.g. "How have you tackled this previously?... How did that approach impact on xyz?*

#8 Pause and question: Another useful stand-by technique is to ask what I call a "pause" question. Literally, take a pause. Conversation doesn't have to be a fast-paced rally; you don't need to match the pace of the return to the speed of the serve.

> **Quick Tip-in-Practice: Pause questions create and acknowledge space.**
> **Pause**. Take a breath.
> **Acknowledge**: *"We've covered a lot of ground here."*
> **Ask – you**: Either *"What stands out for you?"* or
> **Ask – me**: *"Let's take a moment... Okay... (then playback/ask a question)"*

From trapeze to tee At the risk of mixing metaphors (apologies to editor)...

I often visualise the asking of a question in the context of a golf shot.

Hitting the sweet spot – A powerful question is like a perfect drive off the tee – the further the golf ball travels, the further the client's thinking develops as you walk up to the ball together.

Your 200-metre* drive has created uninterrupted space for the client to verbalise their thoughts.

A golf professional once told me: *The secret to great shots is* **confidence**. *Swing confidently, transfer your energy and let the club do the work.*

Choose your club – For the next shot, you pick your club depending on the purpose of the question – does this need a sand wedge to get us out of this thread – or a quick chip up to the green?

What are you trying to achieve with the shot? More distance in the same direction? A change of direction? Your range of clubs is your range of question types and you have a full set. Choose a club which can give you distance, positioning or precision. Or all three.

Walk together – The crucial part is the time spent walking together – the client's thinking time – walking alongside, attentively focused on the client. Not thinking about the shot ahead. Just listening. And walking at the client's pace.

Park the cart – Don't be tempted to jump into a golf cart and chase off after the ball at speed, desperate to take your shot (ask your question). The cart shortcuts the client's thinking. So park the cart.

*Anyone who's ever seen me wield a golf club knows that a 200-metre drive is wishful thinking.

> **Swing confidently** – and let the question do the work.
> **Choose your club** – you have a whole range of questions in your bag.
> **Walk together** – alongside, attentive and 100% client focused.
> **Park the cart** – don't rush the journey to the next question.
> **Use your full set of clubs** – don't stick to your favourite questions.
> Mix it up.

Mixing it up

Let's apply some of the principles and question types through a sample slice of a conversation. Look out for the nugget words and question types.

Coach: *Tell me – how have things developed since we last met?*

Client: *Lots to tell you… situation with my boss is better, but still sticky. And I've been asked to lead a high-profile project which will really give me a chance to make a name for myself in project management.*

Coach: *You said the situation with your boss is "better but still sticky"; specifically what does "sticky" look and feel like?*

Client: *Sticky in as much as he's really making an effort but it's not embedded yet; it feels a bit forced, and we've spoken about it. But it's getting smoother, slowly.*

Coach: *What's the impact of "smoother"?*

Client: *More natural conversations, me being included in stuff, knowing what's going on – and all of that means I can do a better job.*

Coach: *So, the situation with your boss is better, you feel it's getting smoother, which will help you do a better job.*

You mentioned leading a high-profile project which gives you a chance to make a name for yourself in project management. How are those two things connected?

Client: *Well, it's a company-wide project – everyone will see and feel its results. They'll be quick to point the finger if it goes wrong and it's my name that will be in the frame.*

Coach: *What would represent a good result – for you and for the company?*

Client: *Good would be – the project delivers to its full potential and all of my colleagues will quickly see and feel improvements. And I'll be seen to have done a good job.*

Coach: *Your name is in the frame for the good job; what specifically would your bosses – and your colleagues – be saying about you?*

Client: *They'd be saying I've led from the front and delivered on my promises.*

Coach: *And what else?*

Client: *And they'd be saying that I'm a really good project manager – and give me more projects!*

Quick Tip-in-Practice: Consciously label your questions and techniques.
During your post-coaching reflection, identify the types and combinations. How did you transition from one thread to another/ dig deeper?
Labelling helps to embed your techniques and develop fluency.
So you're never left without a question.

Recapping – at a glance

🙶 What if I can't think of a question?

At a glance

- There are lots of questions that could be effective; don't search for "the one".
- Great questions are: Contextual – Connected – Contribute.
- What's your purpose for asking the question? (Explore/clarify/expand).
- Listen for nuggets – create threads from the nuggets – QAQA.
- Use summary to close off one thread and start another using a parked nugget.
- Mix it up – use a combination of wrapped and standalone questions.
- Combine different types of questions from your toolkit:

    #1. Open & closed questions – general exploration. Why not why?

    #2. TED questions dial up the strength of the ask (command).

    #3. Precision words dig for more detail. Specifically, precisely, exactly.

    #4. Expansion questions go wider/expand initial response. What else?

    #5. Missing questions trick the brain to come up with additional input.

    #6. Flip questions to overcome and leverage creative barriers.

    #7. Agile questions are your standby tool. Simple, standalone questions that are virtually content free. There are always four trapezes you can swing onto.

    #8. Pause and question. It's not a race. Take a conscious pause. Silence is okay.

Don't panic. Calm your mind.
You've been asking questions since you first learned to speak. You already have your "Questioning Proficiency" badge.
You have all the tools you need to create great questions in the moment.

Invisible frameworks

Good structure supports great conversation.

The framework is invisibly "**under the sand**" – our client should be blissfully unaware as we move **seamlessly** through the stages.

Structure should enable – not contain – the conversation.

CHAPTER 2
Serving soggy quiche

I've lost count of the number of times that coaches have brought up this topic in our supervision conversations. They'll often say a variation of the following:

- "Session felt flat in the middle – we went round in circles for what seemed like ages."
- "It was hard going – we covered the same ground time and time again without making any progress."

I refer to this kind of conversation as being like a soggy-in-the-middle-quiche; instead of rising in the oven, it collapses into a watery pool – flat, soggy and unappetising.

I'm not a chef – and am uniquely unqualified to give baking tips! – so the question we're going to explore in this chapter is:

> **How can I avoid going round in circles in a coaching conversation?**

Going round in circles – or having soggy-in-the-middle quiche – is a typical symptom of structural deficiency. In my experience, 99% of the time it's down to a missing ingredient within the underpinning framework.

Frameworks – and the invisibility factor

Coaching frameworks are many and varied, and we'll all have our favourite acronyms which we've learned or adapted through our coaching journey.

The role of frameworks is to give invisible structure to the conversation and enable forward momentum towards client-determined action. To enable – not contain – the conversation. (More on this later.)

Most coaching frameworks are "bridging" models – helping the client get from where they are now, to somewhere they want to be. Essentially, the actions taken will help to "bridge the gap" between current and future states.

> **Your framework should be invisible to the client – under the sand.**
> Avoid signposting the stages through your language.
> E.g. Goal, Reality, Options, Way Forward
> *Coaching for Performance* (Whitmore, 2017)

Being aware of the framework during the conversation helps us to structure the session time – and know where to go next. Conscious awareness can easily slip out through your language. I encourage coaches to avoid referring to the stages within your questions.

> **Quick Tip-in-Practice: Use alternative phrases/words.**
> **Using GROW as an example:**
> **Goal** – what would you like to **achieve**...
> **Reality** – tell me about the current **landscape**...
> **Options** – what **strategies** are available/what **routes** can you take?
> **Way forward** – what **action** is needed to **make this happen?**

Keep the labels for each stage in your head. The main reasons for this are:

1. Most acronyms are recognisable as such – the words which denote each stage may sound strange and jarring in what should be a fluent conversation.

2. We don't want to alert the client to the internal process we're applying. The conversation should feel natural and seamlessly "in the moment" – even though the client knows we're applying skills to the conversation, showing the workings may put this feeling at risk.

3. If the client is familiar with the framework, they may start working the model, driving the conversation to the next stage before the current stage has been fully explored – and challenged. (Clients may consciously adopt this as an avoidance tactic to move the conversation out of an area of discomfort or challenge.)

The role of a framework is to support and enable the forward momentum of conversation towards agreed action.

> **Each stage/ingredient contributes to the end result.**
> Missing out a stage is the same as missing out an ingredient –
> the dish may not turn out as you'd hoped.

Enable vs contain

I mentioned earlier that frameworks should "enable" rather than "contain". The framework in our head should be a reference point of stages to cover – in an agile, seamless and invisible way. In the early stages of learning, many coaches – in conscious competence – use the framework to drive the conversation, instead of the other way around. And instead of supporting and enabling exploration, the framework "contains" it.

These conversations are often described by the coach as feeling clunky and mechanical. This is because the focus is on the system, not the client and the conversation. As with any other learning, practice and post-practice reflection help to embed the learning until we reach unconscious competence – that is, doing without thinking. And that only comes with time.

Invisible framework – the key ingredients

Hundreds of coaching frameworks and models have been developed over the years; every coach applies their own labels to the stages of their favourite framework and a new acronym is born. But the grandaddy of all bridging models is Sir John Whitmore's GROW model, which describes the key elements (ingredients) needed for an effective, enabling coaching conversation. First published in *Coaching for Performance* in 1992, the model presents the following elements which we're all familiar with:

Each stage has a clear purpose:

- **G** **Goal** – identifies desired outcome/future state/what good would look like – and clear measures to identify "how we'll know when we've got there"

- **R** **Reality** – explores current situation, problems/issues to be tackled

- **O** **Options** – identifies and critically analyses a range of potential routes/strategies to bridge the gap between the current situation (problem) and the desired outcome

- **W** **Will/Way forward** – pins down the actions needed to deliver the strategy and tests commitment to take the action

Whitmore never intended that GROW should be linear. He envisaged a conversation where the stages might be visited more than once, and not always in sequence.

Quick Tip-in-Practice: F-GROW or T-GROW are popular adaptations.
Focus – where would you like to focus/talk about?
Topic/Talk – what would you like to talk about today?
Goal and Topic are NOT the same thing.

In practice, the addition of an F or a T stage helps identify the scope of focus or attention for the conversation, *e.g. I'd like to talk about my relationship with my manager.* Then we start to explore that, *e.g. "Tell me about that relationship."*

In this example you can see that the coach has moved into the Reality stage – exploring the current state of the relationship: where it's been, how it feels, and how it's impacting.

GROW is versatile – the sequence depends on topic/focus of the coaching.
When problem-solving Reality will often come before the Goal – the client needs to describe the current baseline of the situation before identifying where they want to get to/what good would look like.*
When the client has a defined aspirational goal, the Goal may be explored first.

If we try and go for Goal before understanding the Reality/landscape, the client will start there anyway – they'll answer a Goal question with a description of the situation.

In practice, the GROW model is typically deployed to good effect as:

T/F — R — G — O — W

Arguably, F-RGOW isn't as catchy or easy to remember as GROW – but it does reflect the actual stages of many real-life coaching conversations.

Over the years I've watched hundreds of coaches – and line managers who are developing coaching as a leadership style – battle against the GROW model because:

- they've been taught the model as a rigid sequence; and/or
- they've confused the Topic and the Goal (what the client wants to talk about vs what they want to achieve); and/or
- the model is being used to address an issue or solve a problem.

> **Not all stages are equal. Typical proportions of session time might take:**
> Focus = 2%
> Reality = 45–55%
> Goal = 10–15%
> Options = 25–30%
> Will/Way forward = 10–15%

Don't skimp on Reality. We need to understand the extent of the iceberg – how it formed, how big it is, how it's impacting – not just the tip that's visible above the surface.

> **Quick Tip-in-Practice: There's always more Reality to explore.**
> Dive and test – use directional questions (see Chapter 1).
> There's always scope for one more question.

How soggy quiche happens

Soggy quiche – a session that feels like it's going round in circles – is usually the result of circling between the problem (which sits in Reality) and potential solutions/routes to solution (Options) and back again.

R ⇄ O = 🥧

Human nature is such that – when we're made aware of the Reality of a problem – we want to help; our solutioniser brain is triggered to identify ideas and Options. The circling back and forth between the problem and potential routes inevitably generates frustration and umpteen barriers – because there's no clarity of Goal/destination. Our need to help is driving us to the wrong stage of the framework.

> **Unless we first identify what the client wants to achieve.**
> – i.e. what would a good resolution look like for them in relation to this problem/situation – **we risk solving the wrong issue.**
> Here's a summarised example:

Coach: *What would you like to focus on today? (Focus)*

Client: *The relationship with my line manager has deteriorated significantly in recent months so I'd like to spend some time on my next steps.*

Coach: *You said it's deteriorated significantly in recent months – tell me more about that. (Reality)*

Client: *Newly appointed… trying to make a name for himself… doesn't value what I do… constantly undermining me… had a conversation, not improved… impacting on my confidence and motivation… (Reality – Coach will be testing these assumptions/drilling down into specifics).*

Coach: *So, what can you do to improve the relationship? (Options)*

Client: *Improve it! I'm not interested in putting any further work into it! I've decided to move out of this department and there's a role in another department that I'm really excited about… it's doing the stuff that I love – and it's a great career move.*

As you can see, in this example the coach assumed that the client wanted to fix the relationship. In fact, the client's Goal is to get a new role in another department. Unless we ask a Goal question – between Reality and Options – we risk solving the wrong issue.

Adding the "G" – the missing ingredient

So, we need to insert a Goal into the conversation – after Reality and before Options. In practice there are two sizes of Goal – I call them the "Big G" and "little g".

You might add one or both – it depends on the positioning of the coaching session and whether this is a one-off, standalone coaching conversation or if it's part of a series or wider assignment.

In a coaching assignment (a series of conversations), the Big G – and how to measure when it's achieved – will be pinned down during the contracting conversation (see Chapter 8).

> **Quick Tip-in-Practice: Identify which type of G is needed.**
> **Big G** – relates to the situation/problem (and assignment as a whole) what's the desired outcome/what do they want to achieve?
> **Little g is the session goal**. I call it the "get" – what the client wants to "get", "achieve" or "take away" from today's conversation.

In my view, regardless of whether the coaching session is a one-off conversation or part of a series, we need to understand – specifically – what the client wants to get (or take away) from the conversation. It may be a first step, or a complete strategy. We need to understand their frame of reference, otherwise we risk not delivering on our client's expectations.

> **Identifying a session goal – a "get" – after** Reality **and before** Options **will give focus and momentum to the remainder of the session – and ensure that the quiche rises in the middle.**

The session goal – a "get" – is an essential ingredient

So, how do we go about inserting the session "get" (goal)? Here's my three step tried-and-tested recipe:

1. **Summary** – Acknowledge the end of Reality with a comprehensive summary of the ground that's been covered:
   e.g. "So we've talked about abc and you've mentioned xyz are having a negative impact at the moment…

2. **Time check** – Explicitly look at your watch and see how much time has elapsed and how much time is left. It's your responsibility to manage the session time, so use this opportunity.
   E.g. "We've got 30 minutes left of our scheduled time together…

3. **Get** – Having highlighted the scope and scale of what's been covered, and signposted how much time you have left, now you can focus the client on what – specifically – they want to get from the conversation. This signposting helps to make the goal realistic and focus on priority.
   E.g. "What specifically would you like to get/take away from this conversation"?

You've signalled the end of the exploration (Reality) phase, and identified specific expectations on what needs to be achieved in the remaining time and stages. (Options and Way Forward):

> **Quick Tip-in-Practice: Try out the three-step technique.**
> See how the little "g" lifts the energy and gives shape to the session.

Closing the conversation – tailing off or tying a bow?

The session goal ("get") plays an important part in closing the conversation. You need it to wrap things up. Often I observe coaching conversations tailing off at the end; once the actions are identified, the coach struggles to close the conversation off, and the energy and focus seem to fade. It can look – and feel – awkward.

Instead of letting it tail off, let's finish with a flourish and tie a huge bow at the end of the conversation! We can only do this if we identified a session goal earlier on. This "get" provides us with the loop for the bow. (We can't tie a bow without a loop!)

> **Quick Tip-in-Practice**: **Tie a bow – after the client has verbally recapped their actions, we refer back to the session goal/"get":** "So, you said what you wanted to get from this conversation was x; to what extent have we achieved that?"
> **But remember: No "g" loop = no bow.**

This serves to highlight what's been achieved during your time together – the meeting of expectations – and helps give commitment to the planning of future actions/ sessions.

At a glance – "How can I avoid going round in circles"

- Keep your framework invisible – "under the sand"; don't name the stages.
- Add F or T to the GROW structure to form T/F – RGOW.
- Topic and Goal are not the same thing; GROW is not delivered in sequence.
- Reality MUST come before Goal when problem-solving – you need to know the baseline/current situation first.
- Reality typically takes 50% of time – fully explore this before moving on.
- Two sizes of Goal: Big G (overarching goal relating to content of the assignment) and little g (the session goal or the "get").
- Soggy quiche happens when we circle between Reality & Options – we need a G!
- Three-step recipe to add the missing "g":

1. **Summary** – "*So we've talked about abc and you've mentioned xyz are having a negative impact at the moment...*
2. **Time check** – "*We've got 30 minutes left of our scheduled time together...*
3. **Get –** "*What specifically would you like to get/take away from this conversation?*"

- Finish with a flourish – tie a bow – acknowledge achievement of expectations.
- Use the "get" that you inserted between Reality and Options to make the loop.

Ask vs Give

from the client's perspective

Asking...
invites **exploration**; it **stretches** and **challenges** existing perceptions, inspires **creative problem solving**, and develops **confidence**, **resources**, **resilience** and **ownership**.

Giving...
delivers none of the above.

CHAPTER 3
Slipping out of "ask" gear

At some point in their practice most coaches will encounter this slippage, hence one of the most-asked questions/most requested discussion topics is:

> **How can I avoid giving advice and solutions when I'm supposed to be coaching?**

What does this look like?

This "slipping out of ask gear" might manifest itself in a range of ways;

- "I could hear myself asking **leading questions** to help the client find the obvious solution."
- "I held off for as long as I could, but it was something I knew I could help with so I **switched into mentoring** for a bit."
- "I tried to stay in coaching mode – I really did. But when the session finished, **we took it offline** and I was able to help by giving them some advice."
- "The client didn't have any ideas of their own, so **I helped by sharing** some of mine."

All of these illustrate the coach slipping out of ask gear. You'll notice the common theme here – the intention in each of these scenarios is to "help" the client by "giving" – advice, ideas or solutions.

And whilst the intention is a good one – to help – our role is to enable exploration. Providing a quick fix potentially denies the client that opportunity for exploration and – deliberate use of emotive language here – "stunts" the client's potential growth and resilience.

There, I've said it. As a coach I'm sure that you'd hate the thought that your help is stunting the capacity of your client to solve it for themselves. And there it is.

Whose need are you meeting when you "give"?

> **The greatest help you can give is NOT to give.**
> Asking grows individual capacity, resources and resilience
> Giving stunts the potential for resource, resilience and growth.

Slipping out of coach mode ("ask") and into another mode – whether you call it "offline" or "mentoring" it's still a "give" mode – means you've stopped coaching.

The ask: give relationship

I often illustrate the relationship between coaching and mentoring as an ask:give continuum, with the ratios representing the amount of ask vs give in a conversation.

| 0% Ask | 50% Ask | 100% Ask |
| 100% Give | 50% Give | 0% Give |

Mentoring covers a spectrum; in my view, good mentoring begins at 50% ask and contains specific inputs from the mentor's experience that are useful and relevant to the mentee. It will also contain a proportion of well-framed questions, playback and challenge. The "ask" skills are the same as coaching; it's the level of input that differs.

In coaching, we're helping the client come up with their OWN strategies using a range of skills, tools and techniques. So the ratio of ask is much higher.

Occasionally there may be a genuine, tested need to give an input designed to help the client's creative process, but our job as coaches is to stay as far up the ask ratio as our skills allow.

Giving a single specific input, therefore, doesn't necessarily mean we've slipped into mentoring; it all depends on how it's framed and phrased. (More on phrasing later.)

This is where an awareness of the "ask gearbox" comes into play.

The ask gearbox

Ask – coaching mode

Offer – coaching mode
Suggest – mentor mode
Advise – mentor mode

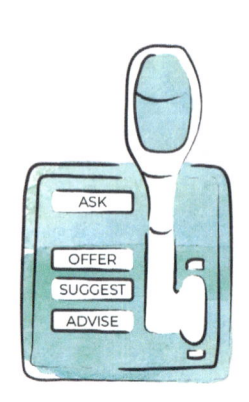

**Tell = directive mode.
Puts client development into reverse.**

Staying in coach mode means using predominantly the "ask" gear. This is your drive gear – it drives the client's exploration and growth. If you need to offer an input to help the client's creative process, switch to **"offer"**. You're still in coach mode if it's phrased correctly.

Why does it happen?

Slipping from "ask" to "give" typically happens for one of the following reasons:

Loss of will – the will to coach is overpowered by:

- your need – to fix/solve/rescue/help. Often this need is rooted in identity – you've always been the "fixer", the "helper" or the one who comes up with ideas. Overcoming your needs for the benefit of the client takes awareness and strength of will.

- your beliefs around coaching role, remit and value. Beliefs are formed from experience and are shifted through evidence. If you hold a belief, for example, that the only way to help is to give, this will shape your coaching style and your ability to stay in coaching mode.

Lack of skill – the skills needed to respond in coaching mode to a "don't know" response from your client aren't sufficiently strong or developed. Your toolkit of idea-generation techniques is empty or – in the moment – you can't remember any.

And you slip from ask to give.

Occasionally it might be down to a **mismatch of need/expectation**, i.e. you've contracted for coaching when the client actually needs – and wants – mentoring. This should be covered at the Chemistry meeting (see Chapter 7) and the scope and remit of your role (as coach or mentor) confirmed during the Contracting conversation (see Chapter 8).

Slipping out of "Ask" gear – be alert to your triggers.
Will – Are your needs or beliefs overpowering the needs of the client?
Skill – How many idea-generation techniques do you have/use?
Mismatch – What level of "give" is needed by the client vs contracted for?

When does it happen?

The danger zone for slipping out of ask gear comes when the client is trying to identify potential strategies, options or solutions – during the Options stage of GROW (see Chapter 2) or or Choices stage of *The Oscar Coaching Model* (Gilbert & Whittleworth, 2009).

T/F   R   G   O   W

During this stage of the coaching conversation the focus is on generating ideas that can help solve or fix the problem. Your solutionising – and helping – responses are triggered and desperate to contribute to the rescue.

Beware the Options quicksand!
Easy to step into, difficult to get out of.

What are your triggers?

Your triggers for slipping into "give mode" may stem from your will to coach being overpowered, or a lack of idea-generation skills – or both.

> **Quick Tip-in-Practice: Identify what triggers your "give" response.**
> Review recent coaching sessions where you slipped out of "ask".
> Was your will to coach overpowered by your own need to help/fix?
> Did your client demonstrate a "don't know"/lack of resources?

Recognising what triggers your give response means you can anticipate and plan ahead, and have a range of appropriate tools and techniques to manage your response.

When you feel the need to "give" bubbling up... some useful tools

Let's start by addressing some of the Strength of Will reasons – when the will to coach is overpowered by your need – to fix/solve/rescue/help – and/or your beliefs around coaching/your role and remit.

Firstly, a need to help and a belief that helping = "giving" are linked; the techniques to address these inner drives will overlap and need reinforcing in order to change the belief and the associated habitual behaviour.

1. Challenge your need: Consciously self-challenging your need (and habit) will help to break the habit and the response.

In this set of self-challenge questions there are four questions:

- Whose need am I meeting?
- How are my needs manifesting right now?
- How are my needs impacting on:
    - Me? My focus is internal now; I've stopped listening and the battle of wills is raging in my head.
    - My client? My focus is away from my client, and my listening is impacted, which impacts on my ability to ask questions...
- Whose agenda am I serving right now?

> **Quick Tip-in-Practice: Tough self-talk – the inner game.**
> Pose the first three needs questions to yourself.
> If your answers involve responses such as "I'm helping the client...
> - because they haven't got any ideas" – see techniques to help generate ideas on page 40
> - because I know the solution/what they should do here" – read on...

2. Spot the signs – If your internal "fixer" is busy generating ideas and solutions to "help" the client, then you may notice some or all of these behaviours:

- **Lots of internal noise** – specifically internal chatter which is focused on "what they **should** do... what they **need** to do... what they **could** do is... Be alert to the language in your head.

- **A feeling of excitement** as your internal problem solver identifies "the" solution, and you can't wait to share it.

- **Are you listening or waiting to speak?** – Literally bursting with excitement as you wait for the client to finish speaking... so you can tell them **the** solution/your great idea of what they **should** do.

(You might notice that some of the words relating to identifying solutions are emboldened; we'll address the notion of "the" solution and what the client "should" do in the next section.)

Now, whilst some or all of those may be going on internally, they might also leak out into the conversation in the following ways:

- **Clipping the client** – It's not as painful as it sounds. Clipping happens when you ask a question before the client has finished speaking. It "clips" their thought process, as they may not have finished articulating their thinking.

- **Leading questions which are "breadcrumbing" towards a solution** – When you've identified **the** solution – or where you think the client **should** go – the questions you ask may develop into questions which are laying a trail for the client to follow... towards **the best/the obvious/your** solution.

  However subtle you might think you're being it's actually quite easy to spot when a coach is breadcrumbing, as the questions often start with:

  o **Have you...** thought about/looked at/considered... x?

  o **Could you/Would you...** look at/think about/consider/do... x?

  o **Is it... Could it... Would it...?**

Leading questions have to lead TO something – an idea, solution or input.

So if you're using leading questions, then you're no longer in "ask" gear – you've moved into "suggest" gear. Even though you haven't explicitly suggested your solution or idea, you're leading the client to find it for themselves.

Quick Tip-in-Practice: Listen to the first three words of your questions.
Are you breadcrumbing? Dropping clues for your client to follow?
Leading questions indicate that you've slipped out of "ask" and into "suggest" gear.

3. Handling your beliefs – Often it's your beliefs that prompt you to slip out of "ask" gear. Beliefs are the views that we hold, based on what we hold to be true. These views are reinforced – or removed – based on conscious testing and evidence.

Internal dialogue can trigger a shift into "give" mode, e.g.

"I can see what the client should/needs to do… xyz is the right solution here."

"I've seen this before. The best solution for my client would be to do… xyz."

Both of these trigger thoughts are based on the coach seeing, recognising or knowing what the right or best path for the client is in a specific set of circumstances.

#1 Belief: I know what they should/could do…

> **The coach cannot ever fully "know" a client's situation.**
> and therefore what is "best" or "right" for them.
> We know only what is shared – above the waterline and made visible.

Like an iceberg, the vast majority of the issue is hidden from view; whilst the problem, issue or situation may APPEAR to be similar to something we've encountered previously – or the solution may APPEAR "obvious" – only the client fully understands the risks and consequences of the situation. So what we think might be a good or even the best solution, cannot take account of the risks and consequences of any action.

#2 Belief: I've seen this before – I know what to do…

One of my favourite pieces of wisdom comes from Heraclitus:

No man steps into the same river twice, for it's not the same river and he's not the same man.

This refers to the ever-changing dynamics of life. Flowing water is somewhere different – the river has changed. Equally, the man has aged or changed since he last stepped in.

Let's work on the basis that every situation is unique; it may appear – on the surface – to have similar characteristics or appear "the same" as something you've encountered previously. But you don't – can't – know the full picture of the client's journey, risks and implications of doing – or not doing – xyz.

> **Quick Tip-in-Practice: The mental "slap" – Give yourself a strong talking to.**
> When a belief about the value of "**your**" solution pops into your head:
> "**How DARE you assume** that your answer is THE answer, the RIGHT answer or the BEST answer!
> Arrogance and ignorance have no place here."

Joan's story: Slipping into "give"

Joan's battle with "giving" has been ongoing; she qualified as a coach four years ago and is in high demand as an internal coach within a healthcare setting. We'd had numerous conversations around her "getting dragged into mentoring" and "knowing what her clients needed to do." I remember in one supervision she told me: "I had to literally stuff my fist into my mouth to stop myself giving advice."

Joan recognised that her beliefs around coaching were driving this behaviour; her need to help – "helping means giving" – and "I'm experienced so my advice will always be helpful." She identified that her background as a clinician meant that the only way to shift these coaching beliefs was to "trial" a different method and assess the evidence for an alternative approach. She needed practice-based evidence.

The strategy that Joan deployed within her coaching trial was a two-step one:

First, she asked herself **"Whose need am I meeting?"** – she had this written on a scrap of paper in her pocket.

Secondly, she applied a mental slap. **"How DARE I assume that my answer is THE answer! I am not an arrogant person, and this is sheer arrogance."**

We caught up a few months later, and Joan's smile said it all.

"I've nailed it," she said. "I've used the "need" and "the slap" in over a dozen conversations. Whenever I felt the solution bubbling up, I activated the strategy. I made a note of the solution that was in my head, but didn't let it out. As a result of this trial, I've discovered three things:

1. My clients DID have the resources to find their own answers; I'd underestimated their capacity.

2. Without exception, the clients achieved better outcomes from their solutions than if I'd shared mine. Their solutions were far better than mine would have been.

3. I hadn't been 'dragged into mentoring' by the needs of the client; my needs and beliefs were driving my behaviour."

Beliefs drive behaviours.
We all know from working with clients that it's impossible to change behaviours – and make the change stick – without changing the underpinning behaviours which drive them.

Identify and test your beliefs; challenge yourself on sharing your "wisdom" with the **How dare you** slap! Reflect on the risks and dangers of sharing "wisdom" without full context. And let experience and evidence reshape your beliefs.

Slipping out of ask – techniques to help generate ideas

Let's look at the other trigger for "slipping out of ask" – the skills needed to respond in coaching mode to a "don't know" from your client aren't sufficiently strong or developed. **Your toolkit of idea-generation techniques is empty or – in the moment – you can't remember any.**

Every toolkit needs to include a range of techniques that we can draw on when – during the Options stage of the conversation – the client says simply "I don't know." Client-generated ideas and strategies will build confidence, resilience and ownership – and develop creative problem-solving skills.

Idea-generation techniques – build your toolkit

The coach's role is to facilitate the idea-generation process using all available resources. Idea-generation techniques typically fall into one of three categories – each category draws from different resources. Explore each one step by step – 1, 2 and – if needed – 3.

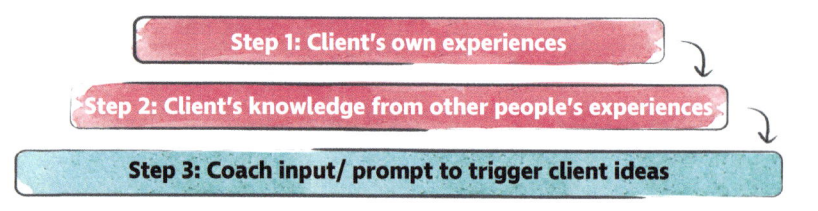

> **Step 1: Client's own experiences**
> **Step 2: Client's knowledge from other people's experiences**
> **Step 3: Coach input/ prompt to trigger client ideas**

> ⚠️ **Explore each category step by step – 1, 2 and – only if needed – 3.**
> Only move to Step 3 when you've 100% tested the client's experiences and resources. Don't skip to 3 without trying Steps 1 and 2 first.

Step 1: Techniques to generate ideas from client's own experiences

#1 Test client'z experience using agile questions

Start the exploration of the client's own experience using one or more directional questions. (See Chapter 1 #7, Agile questions.) Ask questions which direct the client "back" to their past experiences of similar* situations or challenges.

> 💡 **Quick Tip-in-Practice: Test the client's past experiences of similar situations.**
> *When faced with something similar, what's worked for you in the past? How have you tackled similar situations previously?*
> If the client responds with examples of past experiences:
> *... And how could those strategies be useful here/now?*

*This technique relies on the client's recognition of similarities between current and past situations. If the client's response is "This is different" or "I haven't encountered anything like this before", try #2 Characteristics.

#2 Characteristics – tap into client's previous experience

Not every client will recognise the similarities between one situation and another; this prevents the client drawing on their previous experiences to identify options. One way to help the client recognise similarities – and recall previous successful approaches – is to focus on the characteristics of the situation, not the specifics. You may need to include some initial examples to help get the client started.

> **Quick Tip-in-Practice: Focus on the characteristics to help "pattern".**
> Q: *What are the standout characteristics (or hallmarks) of this situation? For example, is it – time pressured/high profile/particularly complex?*
> A: Well, it's complex in that xyz are involved, and I have to lead a matrix team… and we have a really short timescale to get it done.
> Q: *So,* (play back three characteristics): *it's complex, you're leading a matrix team and it has short timescales. Where have you encountered any of these features in the past? What did you do?*

Rule of 3: You'll notice how we've applied the Rule of 3. Three examples generated three items from the client. The Rule of 3 is always super-useful when you're generating ideas.

#3 If… were – what would…? Third person perspective

"If you were giving advice about this to someone… what would you say?"

- This questioning technique is designed to put the client into the shoes of the advisor – from involved participant to detached advisor.

- It helps to detach the client's emotions from the situation – because it's someone else that's (hypothetically) "in" the situation, they can detach from it and take a logical perspective.

- Notice the key words: "If… were" – future forward, and then "what… would you…" There are lots of variations on this, e.g.

"If someone else were experiencing this challenge… what advice would you give?"

#4 Flip question – use a flip question only after original question

When the human brain can't envisage something it creates perceived barriers or a "don't know" response; a flip or reverse question leverages the mental barrier to create an alternative "flipped" perspective. Let the weight of the original question flip it over.

> **Quick Tip-in-Practice: Use a flip question only AFTER asking the original question.**
> Q: How can you approach this? What options might work here?
> A: Don't really know:
> Q: *What strategies or approaches won't be viable here?* or
>   *What ideas or approaches should be discounted?*

Step 2: Techniques for client to generate ideas based on others' experiences

Having established at Step 1 that the client has no experience of their own to draw on, now start exploring external resources – what can they draw from others' experiences?

#5 Seen/observed experience of others

Ask questions which identify how other people have responded to similar situations.

> **Quick Tip-in-Practice: Pose a question to draw on external resources.**
> *When faced with something similar, what have you seen other people do?*
> If the client responds with examples…
> *… And how could those strategies be useful for you here/now?*

If the client response is "This is different" or "I haven't encountered anything like this before", ask a #2 Characteristics question and substitute the follow-up questions with *"Where have you seen others encounter… What did they do?"*

#6 Perceived wisdom – Three wise mentors

Unlike #5 – which draws on observed approaches – this technique enables the client to draw on the anticipated or perceived advice of others (mentors) by requiring them to "be" (role play) that person – walk in their shoes, draw on their wisdom.

The mechanics of the technique are specific and involve the coach taking an active role.

- Opening question: **"If you were to ask three people whose advice you'd value in this situation, who would you ask?"**
- Client identifies three people and tells you who they are, e.g. Martin – my former boss, my grandfather, and… Lord Sugar.
  - Interestingly, clients often include a famous person and/or a revered family member who's no longer available to give advice.
- Coach confirms the names and relationships of each of the three "mentors".
- Coach now **addresses the client** as the first of their chosen mentors, and explains the client's dilemma/problem, e.g.
- *"Good morning Martin. (Client name) is currently facing this situation (describe)…* then the question: *"What is your advice to (client name)?"*
- The coach makes notes of the advice provided, thanks the "mentor" and then repeats the same sequence with the client in the role of the other two mentors.
- The coach plays back the mentors' advice and explores it with the client.

> **Quick Tip-in-Practice: Must identify three mentors – Rule of 3.**
> If the client slips out of character, e.g. "**They'd** say…" then remind them – "You **ARE** (mentor name) – what's your advice to (client name)?"

Step 3: Techniques for client to generate ideas based on coach input/prompt

Taking Step 3 means you've exhausted all of the client-related resources during Steps 1 and 2, and the client is still unable to identify any strategies or options.

Rigorously test the need – This means challenging both your own needs – need to rescue/need to help? – and the thoroughness of your exploration of Stages 1 and 2.

- How sure am I that the client has no further resources to draw on? 10/20/90%?
- How rigorously have I tested those resources? More than one question?
- What are MY needs right now? How are these needs showing up?

> Am I bluelighting when the client has a bandaid in his/her pocket?

Once you're satisfied that the client's resources are exhausted, then it's time to move to Step 3: Giving an input or prompt to trigger client ideas.

Stimulating client creativity – intention and input

The purpose of your input is to stimulate the client's creative process – not provide a solution. We need to develop the client's creative-thinking muscle and stay in coaching mode – so the phrasing of the input is crucial.

Remember the scale of modes in our gearbox:
Ask – Offer – Suggest – Advise – Tell.
Input needs to be framed as an offer.

Framing and phrasing the input – key principles

1. **Position the input**: In order to frame the input as an idea stimulator, pre-position any input to acknowledge the iceberg elements (see Needs earlier in this chapter) before signposting your input and intention.

    Acknowledge the iceberg: *"Every situation is unique..."* Input: *I'm going to share something...* Intention: *to help you create your approach to..."*

    Ask permission. *"Would that be helpful?"*

2. **Give the input**: Be very careful about how you phrase the input.

    > **Quick Tip-in-Practice: Input should be clean and observed.**
    > To avoid the client receiving the input as suggestion or advice:
    > **Describe observed examples** – what you've seen not what you've done. (Even if you experienced the examples, avoid saying "I did xyz".)
    > **Rule of 3**: Always give more than one example

3. **After the input:** The question which follows immediately AFTER the input is the most important element of framing and phrasing as it determines whether the input is received as directive or non-directive,

I.e. Tell – *Advise* – *Suggest* – Offer

Following the input with a statement or a closed question invariably leads to a directive or suggestive mode.

> **Quick Tip-in-Practice: Signpost input as primer – direct to own ideas.**
> **Signpost as primer not solution:**
> *To what extent could any elements of the examples...*
> **Direct to client's own ideas:** *... be helpful in developing your strategy...*

There are literally hundreds of variations that could be applied to these input principles. I'm going to share my all-time favourite, known simply as:

#7 Three pens

I developed this technique during a coaching session; the only props to hand were three pens (well, two pens and a pencil but that's splitting hairs) – hence, three pens.

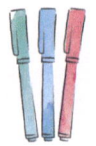

Here's a play-by-play application of the input principles plus the three pens technique.

> ***Coach****: Every situation is unique. I have some examples that might help stimulate your thinking. How would you feel about me sharing these?*
>
> ***Client****: Yes please!*
>
> ***Coach****: In similar situations, I've seen A (describes), I've seen B (describes) and I've seen C (describes).*
>
> *To what extent could any elements of A, B or C be useful in developing your approach to this specific situation?*
>
> ***Client****: Well, I like how A approached it from the other person's perspective and C followed through with an email...*
>
> ***Coach****: So, building on those elements – what might your approach look like?*

> **Input: Observed not experienced – "I've seen abc" and Rule of 3.**
> **Follow-up question framed as idea generator:**
> "To what extent... any elements of... useful in developing your approach?"

Recapping – at a glance

> **How can I avoid giving advice and solutions when I'm supposed to be coaching?**

At a glance

- The ask: give relationship – coaching vs mentoring – grows vs stunts.
- The ask gearbox – asking drives client exploration and growth.
- Different triggers – Will vs Skill – identify your trigger.
- Challenge the need – whose need/agenda? – spot the signs – breadcrumbing?
- Every situation is unique – iceberg (hidden risks) and river – no man enters the same river twice, for it's not the same river and he's not the same man.
- Mental slap: "How DARE I assume that my answer is THE answer…"!
- Build a toolkit of client idea-generation techniques – Steps 1 and 2:

    #1. Test client experience using agile "past/experience" questions

    #2. Characteristics – help the client spot the similarities to previous situations

    #3. If… were… what… would – help client emotionally detach/see it as advisor

    #4. Flip questions – pose the flipped version only after asking the original

    #5. Observed experience of others – what have you seen others do…?

    #6. Three wise mentors – helps client identify advice of others – Rule of 3

- Only give input (Step 3) when Steps 1 and 2 are exhausted. Test the need.
- Position the input: Acknowledge iceberg – Input – Intention – Permission.
- Give the input – observed examples, "seen" not "done" – Rule of 3.

Quick Tip-in-Practice: Check your practice.
What triggers you to slip out of "ask gear" – Will or Skill?
What beliefs do you hold about that slippage?
What action do you want to take?

The client's agenda

Crosswinds are internal distractions which **divert the client's attention** and energy away from the original agenda.

The coach's role is to **notice**, **test** and **determine** their relevance to the **client**.

Crosswinds can pull mental and physical capacity away from the client's agenda – **always test a crosswind**.

CHAPTER 4
Coaching the crosswind

Working with a group of coaches-in-training, I joined a conversation they were having about clients straying off-topic. The contexts and their experiences were varied but the common question being posed was:

> **When a client goes off-topic, how can I get them back on track?**

As I said, within this discussion the coaches shared a range of varied experiences so in this chapter we'll explore what straying off-topic looks like, when it typically happens and some practical techniques for handling the diversion.

Here are some of the examples we addressed within that student session.

1. **#1 Millie** – *"When describing how things were going the client kept veering off at tangents to describe – in detail – things that were happening elsewhere in her organisation. I didn't know whether I should explore these diversions – or try and bring her back to what we were supposed to be focusing on."*

2. **#2 Jon** – *"Right at the beginning of the conversation my client was very specific and said: "Before we start I've seen an advert for my dream job". We'd contracted to work on developing and improving the client's key internal relationships so this would be a signification diversion off-track."*

3. **#3 Sarah** – *"We began the session with the usual update from the client about the actions she'd taken/progress achieved. During the update I noticed a pattern in some of the framing of the responses that she gave: "... given everything else that's going on...", "... despite everything" and "I've done as much as I can, considering..." Do I tackle the "everything else that's going on" or focus on the progress/what we're working on?"*

Three different situations in which the client's attention and energy are diverted away from the original or contracted focus area to describe other topics. The client makes us aware of their existence explicitly – examples 1 and 2 – or implicitly, as in example 3.

We can't know – yet – how important the new topics are to the client. Do they represent general chit-chat? A new priority? Or something else?

> **The client is distracted – their focus, attention and energy are elsewhere.**
> Notice the distraction bubbling through to the surface.
> The coach's responsibility is to notice, acknowledge and test the distraction.

On-track or off-track – the client decides

It's impossible to know whether the new information is connected to the original goal, an emerging new priority – or something else – without digging deeper. If the new topic is:

- likely to **impact** on progress towards the agreed goal; and/or
- a **new priority** that overrides or supersedes the original goals/focus areas

It may be something that the client wants to address and thus needs to be included in their coaching agenda. The coach's role is to help the client test the wind speed and direction. Is it helping or hindering the client?

What is a crosswind?

Crosswinds are things which divert a client's energy, attention and motivation – taking mental and physical capacity away from the original path or goal. Whilst crosswinds are an internal distraction, their presence is made visible through speech and behaviour.

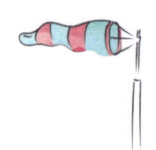

The crosswind concept came to me after a walk on the beach; I'd been trying to walk north along the shoreline, and a strong easterly wind kept pushing me across the beach towards the cliffs. I made little progress until I decided to work with the wind, instead of battling against it. I acknowledged and used its force to support my journey.

The wind blew me along (and up) the beach until I reached the cliffs. In the lee of the cliffs the force of the wind was lessened and I could walk northwards with relative ease. Acknowledging and working with the wind enabled progress towards my destination.

> **Not all new topics will be crosswinds – not all crosswinds need coaching.**
> When a client veers off-topic or shifts attention – it might be a crosswind:
> **Acknowledge – Test windspeed and direction – Coach if needed**

When does a crosswind typically happen?

It can happen at any time in a conversation, or within the wider client assignment.

More often than not, new items emerge early on in the conversation when the client is describing the actions they've taken, and giving you an updated description of Reality (landscape and current situation) which may have new features as a result of the actions taken. These new items literally bubble to the surface of the conversation.

(T/F)   (R)   (G)   (O)   (W)

Listen out for side topics, new topics – and clues to what's NOT being said.

Testing wind speed and direction

When a new topic – or multiple topics – becomes visible we need to establish three things:

1. Test the windspeed – force 9 gale or a gentle breeze?
2. How is it impacting on the client – and progress towards their goal?
3. Does the client want/need to include it in the coaching agenda?

We can establish the above through a series of simple steps:

> **1. Acknowledge (I hear you)** – Summarise the new topic – or the pattern of words that indicate something is diverting the client's attention.
> *E.g. "Let me recap: You've talked about a number of things going on at work... xyz".*
> *"You've made reference to "x", "z" and "z"... (State the cues and clues you've spotted).*
>
> **2. Test windspeed and direction** – Explore the impact of the new topic and clarify if it's linked to the original topic/goal. Use agile questions (up – bigger picture linkage and forward – impact/consequence). Follow through with precision or expansion questions.
> *E.g. "How is this impacting?"*
> *"Specifically what impact is this having on x?"*
>
> **3. Playback** – Summarise the client's responses to the impact questions and highlight any linkage to progress/original goal.
> *E.g. "Okay, so x is impacting on a,b and c... which affect x due to (reasons)..."*
>
> If the new topic isn't a priority/impacting, the summary will help to highlight this. The client may dismiss, *e.g. "It's not relevant to what we're working on/It's a passing issue – I don't need to spend any time on this."* It's a gentle breeze.
>
> **4. Priority to coach?** – Invite the client to determine whether the new topic is a priority to address now or in a later session – or discount it as off-track/ not a priority.
> *E.g. "What are your priorities for today's conversation?"*
>
> If the client wants to discuss now, do a time check: signpost how much session time has elapsed/is left.

Coach facilitates the exploration of impact of new topics.
Client determines priorities and inclusion in coaching agenda.

How – testing technique in practice

Let's apply this approach to the earlier scenarios; the conversation might sound like this:

#1 Millie – "veering off at tangents... describing in detail..."

"I didn't know whether I should explore these diversions" – or try and bring her back to what we were supposed to be focusing on."

Client: Lots to tell you... I had good feedback on my team meeting... there's loads going on... new starter... one of the directors has left... and I've heard that some teams in another part of the business are going to be asked to do overtime...

Millie: So, you had some good feedback about the team meeting. You also mentioned a new starter, a director leaving and that other teams might be asked to work overtime – how do these impact you?

Client: Well, the director leaving – not at all; he's nothing to do with our section. The new starter is great; she needs lots of my time but that's okay – and then the overtime thing; well, that's the biggie really.

Millie: In what way?

Client: As you know, I've just taken over this team and need to make my mark. I've worked with HR to get flexi-working for my team and they love it – and some of them have reduced their hours. We're on top of our workload.

Millie: How is this linked to the potential for overtime elsewhere in the business?

Client: Well, if the other teams don't do overtime to clear the backlog, there's a chance my team could be allocated some of their work, have their hours changed – or have to move across altogether. And I've only just got everyone happy!

Millie: So, you've heard that there may be a need for overtime in another part of the business which – if true – could mean you'd need to make changes within your team when you've just got everyone happy. (Client nods)

We've got an hour left in this session – where would you like to focus that time?

Client: I'd like to spend some time unpicking the overtime thing – it's not confirmed – just a rumour that I picked up. I want to discuss how I'd handle it if it happens. And – if we have time – look at my team meeting, what worked and how I can build on that.

Millie: Sounds like a plan. **Starts coaching the crosswind.** *Tell me – how did you hear about the overtime and exactly what was said?*

Quick Tip-in-Practice: Trust the client:
Client discounted two out of three tangent topics at the testing stage. Client allocated time to the "crosswind" (overtime) and original topic.
The client recognised the need for Millie to coach the crosswind.

#2 Jon – Client is explicit and raises a new topic

"Dream job" – We'd contracted to work on developing and improving the client's key internal relationships so this would be a signification diversion off-track.

> **Client**: Before we start – I've seen an advert for my dream job. It's working for the Superhero team – it's really high profile with multiple stakeholders. I know the hiring manager, so I reckon I've got a pretty good chance. The closing date is this Friday.
>
> **Jon**: So, your dream job has come up; you reckon you've got a pretty good chance – and the closing date is in two days' time – on Friday. How does this impact?
>
> **Client**: I'd need to ask for time off tomorrow to work on the application. I might need to negotiate as we're really short staffed.
>
> **Jon**: You said you'd need to negotiate with your boss for time off; that's one of the relationships you've been working on – how's it going?
>
> **Client**: Well, I'm much better at reading his signals and anticipating what he wants – and what triggers a negative reaction. So I think I'm better placed than I was to negotiate some time off. And I really want to go for this superhero role.
>
> **Jon**: Okay, you're keen to go for the role and you'll need to negotiate some time off with your boss to enable you to prepare the application. (Client nods) We've got an hour left in this session – how would you like to use that time?
>
> **Client**: I'd like to start by looking at the progress I've made with relationships and the techniques I've been using – because I'll need to influence my boss and – if I get this new role – I'll need to build relationships with new stakeholders. Then maybe look at what I want to get across in my application.
>
> **Jon**: Sounds like a plan. **Starts coaching the original topic**...

> **Quick Tip-in-Practice: Lots of ways to test impact and linkage.**
> Coach subtly made the link between original topic and new one (that's one of the relationships you've been working on – how's it going?) Having tested the crosswind, the client's priority was the original topic
> **Not every new topic is a crosswind – or needs coaching.**

#3 Sarah – Implied new topic – pattern of language

During the update I noticed a pattern in some of the framing of the responses that she gave. Do I tackle the implied topic or focus on what we're working on?"

> **Quick Tip-in-Practice: Implied vs explicit – listen for cues and clues.**
> **Sarah** noticed a pattern – the client's phrasing and language suggested something else going on which may be impacting on/a priority for the client.
> **Listen for cues and clues which bubble to the surface.**

Getting back on track – whose agenda am I following?

In trying to get a client back "on track" – whose agenda are you following and whose needs are you meeting? In Chapter 3 we examined the coach's need – to fix, rescue or give a solution.

Here's a real-life example of a coach's needs overriding those of her client.

Marcia's story: The problem client

Marcia booked a call to discuss her "problem client". I asked her to describe the specific behaviours of the client and what made them a "problem" for her. I can remember to this day her exact words:

"This client is a nightmare – we've had three sessions and he's completely non-compliant.

"We agreed in contracting that he'd email me a week before each session telling me what he wanted to focus on the following week. He's only done it once – and even then, the actual topic he wanted to focus on during the session had changed from what he'd sent me a week ago. I can't work like this.

"When I challenged him about it, he just said 'Sorry, I'm really busy – it slipped my mind'. I can't work like this. I can't work with someone who so clearly disregards what's been agreed. I'm going to have to terminate this assignment."

I winced and could feel my toes curling as Marcia described the situation and the "non-compliant" behaviours of her client.

I played back her language, we explored her need for preparation – she felt insecure not knowing what was coming down the track in a session and thus her need to plan the session, prepare some tools and sample questions was all-consuming.

After looking through the lens of the client, Marcia recognised that the client's "non-compliance" was, in fact, clear evidence of their need for spontaneity and freedom to focus on whatever was a priority on the day. Their need (spontaneity) vs her need (pre-planned).

After some reflection, Marcia acknowledged that the "rules" hadn't been agreed – they'd been dictated (by her) – and that her need to prepare and control the process had rendered her oblivious to the client's needs.

Marcia was working to her agenda, not the client's.

Quick Tip-in-Practice – Mental slap – "Whose need am I serving?"
Are my needs dictating – and limiting – my client's exploration and focus?
How DARE I put my OWN needs before those of my client!
My role is to create the space – the client chooses the agenda.

FAQ – Coaching the crosswind

Q: What if the new priority is more important to the client than the original goal we're working towards and contracted for? Do we dump the original goal – or do both?

If – having tested the topic and identified that it's something that the client wants (needs) to work on alongside or **instead** of the original goal – it's important to review and revise the assignment goals. Depending on when the need for revision emerges, it could be approached via a mid-point review (see Chapter 9) or via re-contracting (see Chapter 8). All original stakeholders should be involved in signing off the revised goal and measures.

Recapping – at a glance

> **When a client goes off-topic, how can I get them back on track?**

At a glance

- Off-topic doesn't mean "off track" – new topics may be emerging priorities.
- New topics may be explicit or implied – listen for verbal cues and clues.
- Crosswinds are an internal distraction, diverting attention and energy.
- Test the wind speed and direction; is it a breeze or a crosswind?

   1. **Acknowledge** – Summarise new topics or clues (I hear you).
   2. **Test windspeed and direction** – How does it impact? How does it link to (original topic)?
   3. **Playback** client responses and summarise linkage.
   4. **Priority to coach?** – Is this something the client wants/needs to explore?

Time check – Signpost time available in session/assignment series.

- Test relevance and impact of new topics – priorities that need coaching?
- The need to get the client back "on track" – "Whose need am I serving?"
- Work with the force of the wind – don't battle against it.

Quick Tip-in-Practice: Don't ignore the signs of a potential crosswind.
If a client's attention and focus appear to be elsewhere – call it out. They may resent you for not picking up on their cues and clues and it may undermine their confidence in your coaching ability.
Acknowledge – Test windspeed and direction – Coach the crosswind (if needed)

Dancing in partnership

The client chooses the **dance step** – their step, **their agenda**.

The coach's role is to **match the rhythm and pace** of their partner, and **change tempo** as needed.

Working with the energy of the client and the session time, the coach explores the **full space** of the dance floor…

To deliver **the glitterball moment** – the achievement of the client's agenda.

CHAPTER 5
Pace and flow – Quickstep or waltz?

We've all encountered fast speakers and slow speakers, clients who verbalise their raw thoughts and those who carefully consider every word. The clients who seem to revel in silence – and those who instinctively fill it.

So we're familiar with the many and varied challenges of an effective conversation.

> **How do I speed up/slow down/change direction/get a word in?**

Pace and flow are influenced by:

- speed of speaking – natural patterns and the level of motivation around topic
- internalised vs externalised thinking (think-speak vs speak-think)
- level of challenge – description vs applied thinking needed
- structure and volume of responses.

Pace and flow will vary throughout the stages of a coaching conversation.

When your client experiences a light bulb moment, they're excited and their energy dials up. As their energy transfers from thinking to speech, they speak more quickly.

Conversely, when a client finds a question challenging or is considering the complexities of a situation through applied thinking, responses may be slower, hesitant or paused.

The dance – client leads, coach matches and paces

I often think of a coaching conversation as a ballroom dancing partnership; the client leads and chooses the dance step (agenda). The coach matches the rhythm and pace, anticipating where the music might change and a different step may be needed.

The coach works with the energy of the client – skilfully whirling and twirling, circling back and tackling the high kicks – to explore the full space of the dance floor. The coach manages the time and flow to ensure a full circuit and land directly under the glitterball.

> **The client chooses the dance step – it's their agenda.**
> The coach ensures that the full space of the dance floor is explored – matching pace, changing tempo and working with the energy of the client to achieve the glitterball moment: the achievement of the session goal.

What do we mean by "pace" and "flow"?

Let's use the dance metaphor to explain.

Pace is the tempo – the beat of the music. In a conversation it's the speed of speech and response – question/answer/question/answer – and the energy directed towards it. Too slow and you won't reach your destination – too fast and exploration may be superficial.

Flow is moving in step – naturally and in rapport – the smooth transition from one dance to another, the twirls and changes of direction – without missing a beat. In a coaching conversation, it's the seamless transitioning from one topic to another, from one stage of the framework to the next whilst maintaining a natural flow of connected conversation.

> **Pace**: the tempo/beat of the music – speed of speech and response
> **Flow**: in step – delivering seamless transitions without missing a beat

Pace and flow – the toolkit

There are three primary tools which influence pace and flow; they can combine in limitless ways to deliver different outcomes and support different challenges.

1. Summary

Simply the most super-useful tool, summary is your go-to method for changing pace or flow. Summary can be used to slow or speed up the pace/transition between topics/ change direction – as well as clarify understanding and provide the client with a chance to hear their own words played back. Long answers need more frequent summary.

> **Quick Tip-in-Practice: Use summary as a conscious tool to:**
> **Change the tempo** – summarise more frequently to increase pace
> **Chunk up the client's thinking** – from detailed specifics to headline themes
> **Change direction** – pause and transition to another topic or stage.
> **Clarify and confirm** – client's own words played back.

Changing direction – Let's switch from dance to tennis for a moment.

> **Think of the conversation as a tennis rally: Controlling the ball.**
> Question – answer – question – answer – question – answer...
> Summarising effectively stops the rally (thread of conversation).
> It returns control of the ball to the coach for a fresh serve.
> Baseline or net? New thread or go deeper on this one? It's your choice.

And it's the question which follows the summary which determines where you go next.

2. Question types (and playback)

The type of question you ask can influence the pace of the conversation. Different types of questions can be used to increase or decrease the pace, and encourage the client to think more deeply/from a different perspective. (Refer to Chapter 1 question types.)

Question structure has the biggest single impact on the pace of conversation. Standalone questions pick up the pace, whilst wrapped questions – being slightly longer in their construction and linking back to previous content – slow the tempo of serve/return.

> **Quick Tip-in-Practice: Long, slow answers – I need to pick up the pace.**
> Use more short, **standalone** questions. Open or TED questions work well.
> *What's your top priority?*
> *Tell me about x/Explain x to me/Describe x.*
> *When/where/how does that impact?*

Playback within questions lengthens the "ask" and gives more for the client to work on.

> **Quick Tip-in-Practice: Short, quick answers – I need to slow the tempo.**
> Short answers, a very fast speech pattern, externalised thinking – or too many standalone questions – can impact on the conversational pace. Use **wrapped questions** and questions which require **detail**.
> *You mentioned x; tell me specifically what makes x a challenge right now.*
> *You described it as "nuanced and complex"; what exactly are the nuances?*

3. Your energy – match, mirror, pace

Your energy – and how it's directed through speed of speech – is a powerful pacing tool. To be effective, your speech must be congruent with your non-verbal cues. The energy expressed via body language and facial expressions needs to match your speech pattern.

Matching your energy to your client's energy and mirroring the pace and pattern of their speech and gestures is a rapport-building tool. We do it unconsciously – without thinking.

Having built rapport we can subtly and deliberately use that rapport to change the pace. By speaking more quickly/slowly, using shorter/longer sentences, projecting more/less energy through our body position we change the pace which our client is unconsciously matching. We consciously dial up/down – they unconsciously match and dial up/down.

> **Quick Tip-in-Practice: Match – Mirror – Pace.**
> **Match**: the expression of your energy through verbal and non-verbals.
> **Mirror**: your client's energy of speech, and expressed body language.
> **Pace**: change the pace – dial up or slow down – gently and deliberately.

How do I?... tools in practice

Now let's look at some common scenario-based questions relating to pace and flow.

How do I... handle long detailed answers and lack of focus?

"My client's pace was slow and deliberate – she was carefully choosing her words, and her answers to every question were long and detailed, often reaching back to provide context and description – some of which didn't seem relevant. I was worried that we wouldn't even get to the crux of the issue in the time we had scheduled."

In this scenario the main issue is one of pace. The client appears to internalise her thinking, sharing her thoughts only when she has determined their validity (think-speak). The inclusion of a detailed "back story" means there's additional information which the coach needs to mentally hold and sift for nuggets, and there's a time pressure.

If the coach matches this "andante" pace then it's unlikely the client will fulfil their coaching agenda.

So, the coach needs to address both pace and flow, generate some momentum and identify some clear focus for the conversation.

Quick Tip-in-Practice: Energy – Summary – Question.
Energy – *deliberately mismatch the client's energy during the summary and question – dial up to increase the pace and tempo. (Coach leans forward, positive and engaged energy)*
Summarise – *to chunk up, get out of the detail*
Thanks; you've described the context and journey to your current role...
Question types to use – *short standalone question to move topic*
Where specifically would you like us to focus today?

In this example the coach has moved the client from the landscape description (Reality stage of GROW framework) to the Focus (or Topic). This was deliberate as the issue – or area of focus – isn't yet known in this conversation.

Consciously determine your energy strategy BEFORE any verbal inputs.
Here the coach wanted to deliberately mismatch and increase the pace. Your energy needs to match the words and structures of your speech.

Simple chunk-up technique – Rule of 3

One of my favourite questioning techniques to help clients get up out of the detail is:

- Rule of 3: *"What three things stand out for you/What are the three key themes/What three aspects of this work or don't work/What are your three priorities here?"*

How do I... handle short answers?

"It was hard work. My client gave very short answers and responded really quickly – often only single words. The pressure was on me to keep the ping-pong going – I didn't have time to think of my questions."

In this scenario we're going to assume that the client is fully motivated and that the single word responses are indicators of their thinking/speech pattern.

So we need to encourage the client to give the coach more to work with; single staccato answers deliver very little content and even if every word is a nugget, there's no articulation of the workings behind the answers. We don't have enough to work with.

Both coach and client need more thinking space – we need to slow the staccato pace to a more productive rhythm and use question types which elicit more expansive responses.

> **Quick Tip-in-Practice: Energy – Question(s) – Summary.**
> **Energy** – *deliberately mismatch the client energy and dial down (Coach settles back – relaxed position, calm energy, speaking more slowly)*
> **Question types to use** – *wrapped, precision, agile and expansion questions*
> *"You said x; describe specifically how x fits into the wider context."*
> *"You mentioned y; what's the history behind y – how exactly did it happen?"*
> *"Tell me more about..."*
> **Summarise** – *use summary only after multiple questions and responses:*
> *"You've mentioned how x fits into the strategy, and that y emerged..."*

In this example the coach deliberately used a higher ratio of wrapped to standalone questions (2:1) to slow the pace; the standalone question was an expansion question, which invites expansion of thinking and more detail.

How do I... change direction/start a new thread?

Summarise the thread, and then direct your question to a new nugget or topic. Remember the tennis rally – summarising closes off the rally/thread of conversation and returns control of the ball (conversation) to the coach for a fresh serve.

Your question determines where you explore next.

> **Quick Tip-in-Practice: Energy – Summary – Question.**
> **Energy** – *if pace of conversation is on track, match your energy.*
> **Summarise** – *the thread that you want to finish/feel is exhausted:*
> *"Okay, so we've explored a,b and c, and talked about x,y and x (full detail)".*
> **Question types to use** – *playback and TED (Tell me, Explain, Describe)*
> *"We spoke previously about... tell me more about that."*

Going back to the dancefloor – summarising closes off one dance and enables the seamless transition of the partnership into a new dance or direction of travel.

How do I... get into the conversation?

"I felt like I was standing under a waterfall – my client was speaking really quickly, lots and lots of detail. Absolutely no pauses – he didn't draw breath".

The client's energy is directed towards "getting it all out"; this is often encountered during the initial update or Reality phase of a coaching conversation.

This can feel overwhelming. Your energy is likely to focus initially on listening and nugget-spotting, but may become distracted as you internally ask "How much more? When will he/she pause? How can I get into this conversation?" Internal anxieties may impact on your listening capacity and you may miss key points.

Am I listening or waiting to speak?

Check yourself. Before deploying your entry strategy ask yourself:
How is my client best served?
What's the **purpose** of an intervention now? (Is it to clarify/start a new thread?) Or is it to make me feel useful?

Once you've determined that getting into the conversation is serving the best interests of the client and has clear purpose – your main tool is **non-verbal signalling**. Use your body language to give a clear signal of your intention to enter the conversation.

Quick Tip-in-Practice: Transmit your intention to speak.
Non-verbal signalling: *Signal your intention by consciously shifting your body position into an energised stance, leaning forward and nodding.*
Take a visible breath in – this shows you're ready to speak – and make direct eye contact. Bring your hands up – open palms – to signal your opening.
These physical gestures create energy on your side of the conversation and signal your intention to speak.

Then – once you've entered the conversation – apply your pace and flow tools: Energy – Summary – Question in whatever combination is needed.

Quick Tip-in-Practice: Energy – Summary – Question.
Energy – *deliberately slow your speaking speed slightly to dial down their response speed*
Summarise – *the key themes – chunk it up – headlines not bylines*
"You've mentioned a, b and the impact of c..."
Question *which is directly linked to the **purpose** of your intervention.*
"Where specifically would you like to focus/are your priorities?"
"... Anything more to add?"
"What are your three key themes emerging/observations?"

Getting to the glitterball moment

Getting to the glitterball moment means you've sufficiently managed the pace, flow and time of the session to fully explore the client's agenda – and achieve their session goal.

These are multiple simultaneous responsibilities – you're fully present in the conversation, whilst managing the flow of the conversation through the stages of the invisible framework. And – at the same time – you're consciously managing energy to ensure the pace is sufficient for the client to fully explore their thoughts and reach their goal/glitterball ending.

> **Pacing takes practice – review and reflect on your techniques.**
> Where was my client's energy? How well did I pace the session? What tools did I use? How frequently did I summarise? What was my ratio of playback/standalone questions?

Recapping – at a glance

> **How do I speed up/slow down/change direction/get a word into the conversation?**

At a glance

- Coach's role is to manage the pace and flow of the conversation.
- Pace = tempo (speed of the conversation). Flow = in-step, seamless transitions.
- Pace and flow are influenced by three primary tools:

1. Summary – super-versatile can be used to impact pace AND flow:

  o Change the tempo – chunk up – change direction – clarify and confirm

  o Long answers need more frequent summary – increase pace and change flow

2. Question types – use different question types to change the pace:

  o **Slow down**: Wrapped questions, complex or precision questions

  o **Speed up**: Standalone questions, TED questions – keep it short

3. Energy – your energy can change the pace and tempo – dial up/down:

  o Match verbal/non-verbal, mirror client energy to engage, pace as needed

What ifs...

... are abstract conceptualisations.

They enable us to mentally apply new tools and strategies to future scenarios, to **test validity**, and **build skill**, **fluency** and **confidence**.

We learn from realistic scenarios.

Confidence is undermined by "what ifs" that are based on exaggeration, distortion or catastrophising.

CHAPTER 6
What ifs – a pick and mix

Having explored some of the key themes around structural and conversational techniques, it's inevitable that your brain might play these scenarios forward and generates some "Yes, but what if...?" questions.

The role of what ifs...

These "what ifs" are an important part of how we learn. When asking "What if..." we're creating a hypothetical situation in which the coach applies the recommended techniques and principles. By creating – and then problem-solving – "what ifs", the coach is testing applied learning and developing strategies to de-risk potential future situations.

> **Abstract conceptualisation stage appears in most learning models.**
> What ifs can be a powerful enabler of learning – testing out techniques and how they'd work in future situations embeds the learning.

What ifs can disable a coach by creating fantasy scenarios so exaggerated – and unlikely – that the coach is unable to problem solve the scenario. This undermines confidence in applying the tools and techniques – they've lost their validity without even reaching a real coaching conversation. Fear disables the logical functioning and ability to problem solve.

What ifs – Fear and distortion

I vividly remember a conversation I had with my coach many, many years ago. As a young leader in a very challenging system (not to put too fine a point on it, a very macho and sometimes brutal operating environment), I needed to develop sufficient confidence and resilience to hold my ground and lead in my own way.

During the conversation I was seeking to test the feasibility of a strategy, using a "what if..." example in which my brain had amplified the size, height and scale of the potential obstacles. My language was littered with exaggeration and generalisations.

My coach, Graeme, said softly:

"Do you know what fear is? **FEAR is Fantasy Expressed As Real**.*"*

My learning was instant and blinding.

I wasn't testing the strategy – or applying the learning; my "what if" scenario was completely unrealistic – a fantasy – and generated by fear.

Remember how the mouse in *The Gruffalo's Child* (Donaldson, 2004) used back-lighting to create a giant mouse to scare his predators? Back-lighting your scenario distorts reality and creates FEAR.

In this chapter

We'll explore a range of "what if" questions relating to the ground covered in Part 1, using scenario-based questions created by coaches over the years to test out their learning. Hopefully some of the questions, tips and tactics fit the "what ifs" being generated in your head.

What if... I notice a "nugget" and forget to explore it – or don't have time to explore it?

It happens. The most important thing is that you've noticed the nugget (see Chapter 1) and the opportunity it represents. As long as you capture it and pop it somewhere safe (in your notes) then you haven't missed the opportunity – you've saved it for later.

- If you're aware of it before the session ends and there's insufficient time to explore it, signpost it "You mentioned x earlier; shall we pick that up next time?"

- If you remember it afterwards – when writing your notes or reflections – make a note to pick it up at the next session. A nugget from a previous session can provide a seamless entry into your next conversation.

> **Quick Tip-in-Practice: Nuggets can be saved for later exploration.**
> Either signpost it for the next session or use it as a seamless starter into your next conversation.
> "You mentioned x in our last conversation; tell me more about that."

What if... my mind goes blank and I can't think of anything to say?

Summarise. Summary is our go-to all-purpose Swiss knife; it serves a multitude of purposes and – in this situation – can be used to good effect in a couple of ways:

1. Coach summary: Buys you some thinking time and helps recall the various threads from which your next question can emerge.

Or – hand the baton over to the client:

2. Invite the client to playback their noticings/highlights/emerging themes.

> **Quick Tip-in-Practice: Invite the client to playback.**
> "We've covered a lot of ground/There are a number of themes here...
> What are your noticings/highlights?
> What's emerging for you from the conversation so far?"

💬 What if... my question doesn't land?

Firstly – how do you know it hasn't landed?

If the only visible indicator is silence

The client may be thinking. Remember – the purpose of a question is to invite thinking. If the client internalises their thinking, then your question may well have "landed".

The power of a question lies in its relevance and timing. I referred to this in Chapter 1:

Hitting the sweet spot – A powerful question is like a perfect drive off the tee: the further the golf ball travels, the further the client's thinking develops as you walk up to the ball together. Your 200-metre drive has created uninterrupted space for the client to verbalise their thoughts.

Don't be tempted to jump in and reframe just because the client doesn't answer straight away, e.g. *"What I mean is..."* Coaches often reframe using multiple examples, thereby giving the internal thinker more questions to work on!

Park the cart – Don't be tempted to jump into a golf cart and chase off after the ball at speed, desperate to take your shot (ask your next question). The cart shortcuts the client's thinking so park the cart.

So, ask the question – and leave it. Walk to the ball.

If the client gives verbal or non-verbal indicators

If – after holding the silence – the client expresses verbally or non-verbally – that they haven't understood the question/want clarification – then add clarifying detail.

> 💡 **Quick Tip-in-Practice: Add clarifying detail using precision words.**
> Be careful of reframing a question and dumbing down its impact.
> **Add precision words** to clarify the scope of the question – its specificity:
> Original question: *"What are the consequences of doing x?"*
> Clarified question:
> *"What are the specific consequences for you of doing x?"*

Adding clarifying detail isn't the same as reframing the question. It's holding to the original question. Then – if there's no response to this clarified question – just ask, *"So, what are you thinking?"*

> ⚠️ **Not all light bulbs appear in our presence.**
> Not witnessing an output doesn't mean there isn't one.
> **Rattle questions** – the questions which go round and round in your head. Your client may well bring the answer to your next conversation.

66 What if... the client asks "What would you do?"

It's not uncommon for a client to ask this direct question, particularly if the issue they're struggling with is something they know you have experience of.

What not to do

#1. Push back and remind the client about the nature of coaching
"My role as coach is to help you find your own answers and solutions."
Or *"My experience isn't relevant..."*

This is extremely frustrating for the client and can shift the dynamic of the conversation. The client may feel that you do know what they "should" do and are deliberately withholding help. Whilst reminding the client about your role/role of coaching might feel like a "proper/textbook" answer it's rarely a productive response for the relationship.

#2. Take it offline – *"Look, whilst we're in coaching mode I can't tell you. But we'll pick up at the end of the session/take a time out and I'll switch to mentoring".*

This approach undermines the value of coaching and encourages the client to collude in a covert discussion. And it's high risk as it implies that the coach has the answer to their problem. (See Chapter 3 – every situation is unique.)

Both of these approaches can impact on the trust and dynamic of the relationship.

What to do

Just because the client has invited your input doesn't mean you should slip out of "ask" gear. The approach below applies only when you've fully tested the client's own resources – see Chapter 3 – and are 100% sure that an input is needed to help prime the client's thinking.

Quick Tip-in-Practice: Refer to Chapter 3 for principles.
Respond to the direct question (What would you do?) *"I'd tap into previous experience."*
Position the input:
"Every situation is unique and carries its own risks and context."
Describe multiple examples – what you've seen not what you've done.
"In similar situations, I've seen people do a (describe), b (describe) and c (describe)." (Always give more than one example.)
Signpost as primer not solution:
"To what extent could any elements of these examples...
Direct to client's own ideas:
... be helpful in developing your approach to this situation?"

💬 What if... the client hasn't completed ANY of the actions from the previous session?

Without action there's no traction – the client's Reality (and problem) remains the same, unchanged since the last time you explored it. Same context, same issue, same impacts.

So what happened to the actions the client committed to take? Did they forget or encounter barriers? The coach's role is to test and challenge non-action in an adult–adult state. (See Chapter 9 regarding "Drag factors" and how to handle them.)

Parental-style questions such as "So why haven't you...?/Why didn't you...?" inevitably result in a child-response version of "the dog ate my homework".

> **Quick Tip-in-Practice: Focus on impact of non-action, not excuses.**
> *"So last time you identified three steps you were planning to take. How does not taking those steps impact on your rate of progress. What's the impact of not taking those steps?"*
> Ask adult impact (forward) questions (see Chapter 1).

💬 What if... we spend the whole session in Reality?

Spending a large proportion of the time in Reality – understanding the context/how the client came to be where they are right now/what the current issues are and how they're impacting – can happen in the early stages of a coaching series/assignment. (See Chapter 2 for typical percentage of time for each framework element.)

Managing time and pace is the coach's responsibility, so it's about being aware of the time and framework without compromising the client's needs within the conversation.

If you're nearing the end of a conversation and you're still in Reality – go for action (W of GROW). Without action there's no traction and you risk replaying the same conversation next time. So we need to insert some quick "So what?... What next?" questions to generate action.

> **Quick Tip-in-Practice: So what? – What next?**
> **So what?** Ask the client to playback what – for them – are the key threads or insights gained from the conversation:
> *"What are the key themes/threads emerging for you...?"*
> **What next?** Now link to action with a Rule of 3 question:
> *"What three actions can you take before we next meet?"*
> *"Tell me three next steps you can take."*

❝❝ What if... the client brings crosswinds and we can't get to the agreed agenda

Firstly, check that the crosswinds really ARE crosswinds – see Chapter 4 on how to do this. If there genuinely is a recurring pattern of things which are impacting on the client's intended path – then my #1 coaching adage (Surface – Discuss – Agree) applies:

> **Quick Tip-in-Practice: Surface it – Discuss it – Agree a way forward.**
> Playback your observation as a noticing plus impact:
> *"I'm noticing that new content has emerged in each of the last three meetings...*
> Highlight impact and link to overall progress/assignment:
> *... which means that we've not spent any time on xyz."*
> Signpost to remaining time and invite discussion:
> *We've got x hours/sessions left in our coaching schedule; let's review where we're at, agree your priorities and focus for our remaining time together."*

See Chapter 9 for a typical mid-point review framework.

Remember: You can initiate a progress review/review of focus areas at any point. If the pattern of crosswinds is there – surface, review and agree a way forward.

❝❝ What if... my client arrives distracted, and says they'll need to cut the session short?

I'm sure most of us have experienced this: your client rushes into the meeting, downloads about all the stuff that's going on for them, and says:

"I can only spare x minutes today so can we finish at y time?"

> **Quick Tip-in-Practice: You have two options to consider.**
> **#1. Agree to work within the revised timings** – accepting that the client may not be fully present. Their use of the word "spare" may indicate that this conversation is not a priority for them.
> **#2. Offer the time back/to reschedule** – if it's a virtual meeting this may be more feasible than one you've travelled to get to. I usually frame the invitation in the context of their pressures, e.g.
> *"If you had the whole of today's session back, what could you achieve?"*

If you do agree to reschedule, make sure that the timescales are realistic and take account of the client pressures outlined. Otherwise you risk a repetition, or starting a pattern of cancellations and postponements. See Chapter 8 for contracting.

Using "what if" scenarios to support your practice...

Creating abstract conceptualisations – our "what ifs" – can be super useful in preparing for a coaching session. They can help us to anticipate potential issues, prepare our toolkit and build confidence.

As long as we make them realistic and relevant to the client-specific situation. (Unrealistic or "fantasy" scenarios can create fear and undermine confidence.)

> **Quick Tip-in-Practice: Create your potential "what if" scenarios.**
> How does the conversation usually flow with this client?
> Where have I encountered sticky points in our conversation?
> When have I felt at risk or unprepared?

Then test and challenge the realism and relevance of your "what ifs":

> **Quick Tip-in-Practice: Testing my "what if" scenarios.**
> How realistic is this scenario in the context of this client/relationship?
> What's the percentage likelihood of it happening?
> To what extent am I distorting or exaggerating?

Finally – self-coach your responses:

> **Quick Tip-in-Practice: Self-coach to build strategies and confidence.**
> What are the characteristics of this situation?
> What makes it the same/different to others?
> What tools and techniques do I have in my toolkit to handle this?

At a glance

- What ifs = abstract conceptualisation. This is a key part of the learning cycle.
- What if scenarios help us to anticipate, prepare and be confident.
- What if scenarios need to be realistic and relevant – and client specific.
- Create – Test & challenge – Self-coach your approach to the "what if".
- FEAR = Fantasy Expressed As Real – distorted and exaggerated catastrophising.

If you have a specific "what if" to pose, please scan the QR code in Part 3 to email your question. Whilst I can't respond individually, you may find your question answered in one of my webinars and podcasts – or in a future article or book.

The Coach's role...

... is to navigate in a sea of complexities and hold true to the client's North Star.

PART 2: THE BIG PICTURE
Managing the relationship, managing the assignment

This part of the book explores some of the key questions relating to the practicalities of managing a "formal" coaching assignment – how to get the relationship started, how to maintain momentum, and then finally, how to close the relationship in a way that recognises and honours the partnership.

The client/coach relationship is after all a partnership; as coaches we're responsible for managing the underpinning frameworks, ensuring that our practice is safe and effective. We also need to make sure that we're managing the contact time within the assignment to deliver best value. As for our clients, they need to bring the content on which to build our discussions – as well as the motivation to stretch their boundaries and a commitment to taking action.

> **Trust is the glue that holds the partnership together for the duration of the journey.**

Whether you're working within an organisation or as an external coach, managing the assignment requires you to navigate a sea of complexities in which you – as the coach – are expected to demonstrate an understanding of the currents and hold true to the client's North Star.

The four stages of the assignment

The overarching assignment – when viewed at a macro level – contains a series of recognised stages and specific meetings, each with a designated purpose. Each conversation plays a role in the overall assignment and supports the formation of a strong and productive relationship.

The following chapters will look closely at the four key stages of the assignment in turn: **chemistry**, **contracting**, **review** and **closing**. Facilitating each of these meetings fluently demonstrates professional "polish" and instils client confidence.

Chemistry + Contracting + Session 1 + Session 2 + Session 3 + Session 4 + Session 5 = Close

Mid-point review

Chemistry is...

... a two-way sampling of **flavours**, exploring the client's menu, testing their **appetite** and checking how our flavours **work together**.

CHAPTER 7
Chemistry – sampling the flavours
One of the most frequently asked questions is:

❝❝ How do I run a chemistry meeting?

Before directly addressing the "what" and "how" – what goes into a chemistry meeting and how to run it – let's briefly explore the "why" and the "when" – the purpose of the meeting and when exactly it happens within the wider coaching assignment.

Purpose and positioning – the why and the when

It's generally accepted that the role of this initial meeting between potential coach and client is to facilitate an introduction. Essentially, you're checking whether you can work together, and if the "chemistry" can support and enable an effective coaching partnership.

The chemistry meeting forms part of the "matching" stage within the macro coaching assignment. Typically, the journey starts with an identified individual **need** for development, where coaching is deemed to represent the most effective route.

The next stage is usually to identify available coaching **resources** (from an internal or external pool*) which can potentially meet the need, and then the **matching stage** gets underway.

Need + **Resource** + **Matching (chemistry)**

Within a coaching assignment the matching of coach and client can take place in one of two ways:

1. Client is **assigned** a coach (from a pool* of available coaches); or
2. Client **chooses** their coach (from a pool* of available coaches).

*The pool may be internal (e.g. from a register of accredited/trained coaches) or external (e.g. coaches who have been approved to provide coaching) to an organisation.

Sometimes organisations may use automated preliminary matching – where the system matches information provided by the client with coach details (such as coaching specialisms, geographical area etc) and assigns a coach based on the match of data. Although this preliminary "data match" can be useful in shortlisting potential coaches, we still need to check whether the relationship can work.

That's where the chemistry meeting comes in.

If the client is choosing their coach, it's good practice to provide access to a range of coach profiles and then to encourage the client to choose two or three coaches who they'd like to meet for chemistry checks.

They're always positioned as two-way, no-obligation meetings. The purpose is for the client to experience different coaches and their styles of conversation and to help both people get a feel for whether they could work together in an effective coaching partnership.

> **How does this feel?**
> **What am I feeling, noticing and experiencing?**
> **Could we do some powerful work together?**

Irrespective of whether the coach is assigned to the client – or chosen by the client from a series of chemistry meetings with different coaches – the client typically has four main considerations in this chemistry conversation. You can remember these as the **Four Cs of Chemistry**:

> **Communication style** – Do I feel listened to? Does the coach "get" what I'm saying?
>
> **Connection** – Does the coach "get" me and what I'm about? Do I feel a level of connection?
>
> **Challenge** – Did the conversation challenge my thinking (in a helpful way)?
>
> **Competence** – Does the coach come across as sufficiently skilled to help me?

The fourth element – "Does the coach come across as sufficiently skilled to help me?" – is all about confidence. While the competence element should be a given if – on paper – the coach possesses the right level of credentials, it's nonetheless important that a client feels confident in the coach's ability to navigate the assignment and deliver best value on the investment being made.

So there's a subsequent fifth client consideration: **Confidence.**

This will be demonstrated through your facilitation of the set-up for the chemistry meeting, as well as during the chemistry conversation itself. Showing that you're familiar and fluent in delivering the elements of the matching stage will help build client confidence.

And even if you already know the client – for example, if you work for the same organisation – undertaking a chemistry check will help you to demonstrate another facet of your skillset and help differentiate the "work you" from the "coach you".

So... back to the question:

How do I run a chemistry meeting?

Having covered off the when and why of a chemistry meeting, let's take a practical look at what the actual conversation entails.

Structure and content – the what and the how

Let's start with the practicalities: a chemistry meeting sits outside the macro assignment; it's a preliminary meeting which is usually shorter than contracting or coaching sessions. It's typically between 30 and 45 minutes long and can be undertaken in person, by video call or even telephone.

Before you reach for your logical arguments, let me qualify those points around timing and format.

Timing: The chemistry meeting is not a part of the contracted assignment – it's a preliminary conversation that's about getting to know your client and finding out a bit about the areas they're looking to explore.

If your typical coaching sessions are going to be roughly between 60 to 90 minutes long, then 45 minutes is perfect for the chemistry meeting. The skill in a chemistry meeting is to demonstrate your coaching style – and in doing so help the client find some new insights – without actually coaching the topic forward.

> **Any longer than 45 minutes and you may be tempted (or expect?) to start coaching the client when it's not ethical or appropriate to do so.**

Chemistry is pre-assignment and usually not charged for.

You're not in partnership until you agree and contract to work together – that's the next stage of the macro assignment.

> **The chemistry meeting is a two-way sampling of flavours, exploring the client's menu and testing their appetite.**

Format: You may be sceptical about how much chemistry can really take place via the phone or on a video call – surely it's much better to meet in person? How can you get a feel for the relationship unless you're both in the room?

Whatever your own preferences, it's worth remembering that the world has adapted since the pandemic; working from home has become more established and accepted, and has upskilled all of us in reading cues and clues via a range of mediums.

> **Three years ago, I'd have advocated meeting for a chemistry check in person if at all possible.**
> But now, the laboratory evidence (based on hundreds of chemistry calls conducted by video call) suggests that facilitating a chemistry check via Teams, Zoom or your platform of choice can be equally viable.

In fact, having a bit of distance and control over their own environment can give clients greater confidence. You may find that virtual meetings actually enhance the openness and candour during the conversation.

And in this post-pandemic era, some people may simply not want to meet in person; we need the client to be "with us" in whichever way suits them best.

> **Meet in whichever format works best for the client.**
> It's their choice.
> It's not about your preference.

Can I do a chemistry call by phone – or audio only? In my view – yes, it's doable. After all, when one sense (sight) is removed from the equation we instinctively dial up the other senses.

I often encourage coaches to vary the formats of their coaching delivery and notice the differences. Invariably they describe hearing more when coaching by phone/audio only and – if we've seen the person previously – we can "hear" their subsequent mannerisms.

Try it out – you'll hear the smile, the frown, the shake of the client's head. Our senses are remarkable in replacing one missing input with another.

> **Let's not rule out a chemistry call by phone or audio only.**
> While requests may be rare – most potential clients will want to see what you look like and match your profile with the real person – it is feasible.

It's important for coaches to be able to connect in a variety of ways – and to practice interacting with clients across a wide range of media. We need to be fluent and confident in whichever format our client wants to work in; it's their choice.

Remember, you can always agree to meet in person or by video call for the contracting conversation, if that's what suits the client.

"How do I run a chemistry meeting" is one of the top three questions posed by coaches.

The chemistry meeting should bear the same hallmarks as your other coaching conversations – with some subtle differences.

It's an opportunity for you to demonstrate your style, energy and unique "flavours" within this 45-minute conversation. Plus, it gives the potential client a lived experience of what it would feel like to work together.

You're giving an authentic snippet within a clearly boundaried conversation.

Content – what to cover and how to run the meeting

While no two chemistry meetings will be identical, there is a set of outcomes that are consistent for every chemistry meeting – regardless of whether it's with an internal or externally sourced coach.

> **Key outcomes to achieve**
>
> 1. Facilitate introductions: get a sense of each other and a potential partnership.
> 2. Establish/check the client's frame of reference: what do they think coaching is?
> 3. Explore the client "need": what's their top-level need and main area(s) of focus?
> 4. Identify the level of motivation/driver for the coaching (sent or requested?).
>
> The above outcomes will…
>
> - enable the client to assess the four/five Cs (communication style, connection, challenge, competence – plus confidence)
> - provide an opportunity for you to demonstrate your style and flavour.

Let's explore these outcomes further and consider what they might look and sound like.

1. Facilitate introductions

The first outcome seems pretty straightforward, but facilitating introductions is one that coaches can often get wrong.

Jamie's story:

Jamie is a very experienced and talented coach who I worked with several years ago.

During supervision he used the phrase "always the bridesmaid, never the bride" – making reference to the fact that he'd been invited to lots of chemistry meetings but had never been chosen for the coaching assignment. So his profile was attracting clients, but something was going wrong at the chemistry meeting.

We decided to explore this pattern, and I asked Jamie to reconstruct his "standard" approach to chemistry meetings.

It became apparent that once he had built great initial rapport with the client – the usual social chit-chat – he would then start talking about himself and his coaching track record, areas of expertise and some of the methods he uses.

Jamie explained that he felt the need to prove why he was the best coach for the assignment and – as his desperation grew – he recognised that he was inserting more and more "about me" content into the conversation. It wasn't really a conversation; it was a sales pitch.

Jamie's lightbulb moment came in a flash: "I'm making it all about me; it's not about me!", he reflected.

We identified that Jamie rarely found out much about the client's needs, their coaching topic or what had prompted them to seek coaching.

Having had his lightbulb moment, he set out to try a different approach – facilitating exploration of the client's "stuff" through the use of just two base questions.

Jamie contacted me some months later with an update: he'd been chosen to coach all five of the potential clients that he'd met for chemistry sessions. No longer the bridesmaid, Jamie had flipped his focus from "it's all about me" to "it's all about you".

> ⚠️ **The chemistry meeting is not about you; it's not a sales pitch and the client does not want to hear about your past experiences or what makes you different.**

Potential clients have already read your bio or profile, and you've passed the "I'd be interested to find out more" test. So don't fill the space with your needs.

Chemistry is all about creating the time, space and opportunity for the client to share a bit about themselves. It's an opportunity for the client to experience – on a smaller scale – the thinking/talking space of a coaching conversation. How it feels and what emerges for them.

Your focus should be on their agenda – facilitated through effective questioning, attentive listening and accurate playback. The client hears their own words played back accurately – without judgement – in a safe and confidential space.

Which brings us to the issue of **confidentiality**.

Even though the chemistry meeting sits outside the formal, agreed assignment – you've not yet contracted to work together – ethical practice requires us to treat the chemistry conversation as confidential.

You must make this explicit and clear to the client before they disclose anything which needs to be boundaried.

Immediately after the rapport-building and social pleasantries, I usually introduce the **purpose** of the meeting (after all – the coach is experienced at chemistry meetings, and the client probably isn't) and set the boundaries of **confidentiality**.

> E.g. *"As you know, the purpose of today's call/meeting is to get to know each other, find out a bit about the areas you might be interested in exploring, and to get a sense of whether we might work together.*
>
> *"As with any other coaching conversation, everything we discuss today remains confidential between us."*

Every coach will have their own version of a confidentiality statement.

My preference is to place it immediately after setting out the purpose of the meeting. It emphasises the two-way nature of the chemistry check and closes down the (potentially uncomfortable) notion of the client choosing (you) from a range of coaches. (More on that later: see page 85.)

Confidentiality surrounds every coaching conversation; by making it explicit we're signposting the safety of the space and encouraging openness and candour.

When talking about confidentiality with coach-students I often refer to an old TV advert for a well-known hot breakfast cereal. In the advertisement the child was surrounded by a glowing red shield, indicating that he was warmed from within by the cereal and thus it was shielding him from the cold. Your clients should feel protected in the same way.

> **Surround every coaching conversation with a "shield" of confidentiality.**
> Make it explicit to the client from the outset.

So far, we've invested in rapport-building (your journey/the weather etc), set the purpose and timings for the call/meeting and made explicit the confidential nature of the conversation.

2. Establish/check the client's frame of reference

Now we need to calibrate the client's understanding of what coaching is – and isn't – and check that what we're offering matches their expectations. This is crucial to the effectiveness of the relationship, and the potential to work together.

If the coach and client are on different pages in terms of their understanding of what coaching is – and isn't –and what's wanted vs what's offered, then the relationship has little prospect of delivering effective outcomes.

For example, if the client wants to learn about x, and is looking for a "coach" to share knowledge and experiences of x, then they may need a different intervention – or a different coach. It's important to be honest if there's a mismatch.

Everyone has their own frame of reference for coaching – based on sport, what they've received throughout their career or what others have referred to as "coaching".

> **Coaching takes many forms – many 1–2–1 conversations are routinely referred to as "coaching" but don't bear the recognised hallmarks of coaching.**

Many coaches routinely send some advance information (a short "About Coaching" document or a link to a short "about coaching" document or weblink) ahead of the chemistry meeting, so that potential clients can reassure themselves that this form of coaching is right for them. Whether or not you send reading material in advance, don't assume that it's been read or that the subtleties of "what coaching is/isn't" are fully understood.

It's important that you can fluently answer questions from potential clients who are seeking clarification at the chemistry meeting (or the follow-up contracting meeting).

> **Quick Tip-in-Practice:** I encourage coaches to work on and finish the two statements below. By crafting the words so that they reflect your language, you can convey the essence of who you are as a coach:
> "Coaching is.../coaching isn't..."
> "My role as a coach is to..."

Try and avoid using published definitions or jargon, e.g. "Coaching is unlocking someone's potential... using a non-directive style."

Hello? What does that mean?

You might have noticed that in Jamie's story he set off to facilitate the exploration of the client's "stuff" through the use of two base questions. (By "base" question I mean a parent question – one which is a starting point for exploration. We drill down from the client's responses.)

Over the years I've distilled the chemistry conversation into a simple two-base-question format, from which we facilitate and explore through further questioning.

The first of these two base questions is a calibration question – to help us understand the client's current frame of reference/understanding.

> **Q1. Have you worked with a coach previously?**
> **or**
> **What's your previous experience of working with a coach?**

You'll notice the deliberate use of "worked with a coach" rather than "been coached"; this helps to imply active partnering rather than being passive/receiving.

Once we've got the client's response, we can test out whether the kind of coaching they've received WAS coaching (or something else), and uncover what specifically worked for them, and what didn't.

Here's a sample conversation using a single base question:

Coach: *What's your previous experience of working with a coach?*

Client: *Well, I was coached in school – basketball – I was on the county squad. The coach was totally focused on winning, and would give instructions enthusiastically from the side of the court. We were really successful.*

Coach: *Okay, so you've had sports coaching where the coach gave instructions; have you experienced coaching in the workplace/since?*

Client: *Yes, my manager arranged a coach for me when I took on my first leadership role. It was really useful.*

Coach: *What specifically made it useful for you?*

Client: *Having the space to think, not rushing my thinking, hearing my words out loud and having someone hold me to account for the things I'd agreed to do.*

Coach: *So, having the space and time to think, hearing your own words and having someone else holding you to account. Anything else that made it useful?*

Client: *Yes, my coach would pick up on words and challenge me on what I meant; that was really useful.*

This example shows that – from a single base question – we've established:

- their frame of reference – what coaching is/isn't; and
- the most useful characteristics – what worked best for them.

And we've created reference points for ourselves about the client's expectations.

The second base question can effectively achieve two of the remaining outcomes for the chemistry meeting and hopefully provide the client with some fresh insights during the exploration:

3. Explore the client's top-level "need" and main area(s) of focus

4. Identify the level of motivation/driver for the coaching

While the first base question was a calibration question to gauge the client's understanding and expectations of coaching, this second base question is an open exploratory question.

> **Q2. What's prompted you to look for a coach right now?**

In our laboratory I've observed that clients' first responses typically fall 50:50:

50% start by giving context: they describe their journey to this point, give a baseline (where I am now), and describe the broad areas of focus for the coaching.

50% start off by explaining the trigger: they explain how they identified the need for coaching (a development centre/feedback/not getting a role etc).

Whichever way the client responds, this part of the conversation is very much an exploration of the current landscape; if you're familiar with the GROW model (Goal, Reality, Options, Will), this is the Reality stage plus a high-level gap analysis. (See Chapter 2 in Part 1).

The skill lies in holding the exploration at Reality and asking questions from different directions; although we don't coach it forward, the facilitated exploration and use of playback usually generates some new insights for the client and their areas of focus.

> ⚠️ **An effective chemistry meeting adds value and fresh insights.**

It's important to facilitate exploration around both elements – the stated (what's prompted you to seek coaching) and the implied (where are you now/what's the coaching need?).

This base question provides fertile material for some exploration. Here's a sample snippet using the second base question and a few follow-up questions:

Coach: *What's prompted you to look for a coach right now?*

Client: *I attended a leadership development centre – which was really stretching – and in the debrief afterwards we looked at my gaps and potential development areas. The facilitator who went through my feedback with me suggested that coaching would be helpful, so here I am.*

Coach: *So you've had feedback from a development centre that you found stretching; what specifically made it stretching?*

Client: *Um. It was really fast-paced; we didn't get much prep time and I felt really on the spot. The worst activities for me were the group influencing – where I just couldn't think of the arguments quickly enough – and the individual presentation. My presentation was fine – even, I'd say – good – but I struggled to handle the Q&A.*

Coach: *Okay, so you've mentioned that the lack of prep time and of feeling on the spot made it stretching; and this impacted on your ability to respond to questions and frame responses. What specific development points did you discuss in the debrief?*

Client: *We talked about building a toolkit of techniques that I could draw on so that I'm more confident in handling these "on the spot" questions and making my points. I've taken on a new leadership role and I'm often in meetings where I need to handle questions and influence effectively.*

Coach: *How effectively do you influence in these meetings at the moment?*

Client: *Actually, I'm not effective in the meetings at all; usually I think of the arguments afterwards and I could totally kick myself. But the opportunity is already lost.*

Coach: *Let me check that I've understood (summarise back).*

This example illustrates "trigger-first"; equally the client might have started off talking about their appointment into a new leadership role, what they're noticing about their effectiveness in influencing and then the coach would probe further on the "prompted... right now" element.

> **Quick Tip-in-Practice:** The deliberate inclusion of the phrases "what's prompted" and "right now"
> helps us to identify the drivers and potential motivation for coaching. Has the client requested coaching – or have they been "sent"?

As well as identifying the motivation and areas of focus for the coaching, exploration of this base question gives us a sense of the potential size and structure of the coaching assignment. Is It a main dish or a series of microwave snacks?

Recapping – at a glance

All of the outcomes for a chemistry meeting...

1. Facilitate introductions/get a sense of each other and a potential partnership

2. Establish/check the client's frame of reference – what is coaching?

3. Explore the client's top-level "need" and main area(s) of focus

4. Identify the level of motivation/driver for the coaching (sent or requested)

... can be achieved by asking just two base questions:

Q1. Have you worked with a coach previously?
or
What's your previous experience of working with a coach?

Q2. What's prompted you to look for a coach right now?

> **Quick Tip-in-Practice:** I encourage coaches to craft these base questions so that they sound "like you"
> – reflecting your style, your language, your signature.

Develop your version of these base questions.

This will...

1. enable the client to assess the four/five Cs (communication style, connection, challenge, competence/confidence)

2. provide an opportunity for you to demonstrate your style and flavour.

And – really importantly – these base questions give you both a sufficient "feel" for the partnership potential of this relationship.

This is – after all – a two-way chemistry check.

Closing the chemistry meeting/call

How we close off the meeting will vary depending on whether the client has been assigned to the coach (this is a one-coach check), or whether the client is choosing their coach from a shortlist (meeting two or three coaches for chemistry). The way that the coach handles the closing provides a clear indicator of the coach's style, competence and commitment to ethical practice.

> **The close is your signature.**
> Be mindful of phrasing and framing.

Key points to cover typically include:

- Summarising the purpose of the meeting and its outcomes; and
- Offering an opportunity for the client to find out more (about you/the way that you work). Sometimes this will prompt a "next steps" question.

    E.g. "So we've talked about what's brought you to coaching and explored some of the key areas you'd like to focus on. Is there anything you'd like to ask me?"

- Giving feedback – level of openness/flow of conversation (the "how").

    E.g. "Thanks for being so open and candid; your choice of words and the way that you've described things has given me lots to work with – some really rich language and patterns to play back and explore with you."

- Thanking the client and signposting next steps. This is where careful thought and language is key.

Here are some examples of the "thanking and signposting next steps" elements:

Option 1: Coach has been assigned: We want to give the client time to think; raise the option of meeting with another coach; and signpost what happens next.

E.g. "I've really enjoyed our time together, getting to know you and what you'd like to work on. Hopefully this chat has given you a flavour of how our conversations might feel if we were to work together. I feel confident that we could create a strong partnership and do some great work around xyz. **(Say this if you mean it!)**

"It's important that you have confidence too and feel that you can get real value out of the relationship. So I'll leave it with you; if you'd like us to move forward, then let me know and we'll put some time in the diary for a set-up meeting. This is where we'll pin down the specifics around what you want to achieve and how we'll work together.

"Equally, if you're not sure or would like to chemistry check with another coach, that's fine too; speak to (coaching co-ordinator) and they'll make arrangements.

"Rest assured that everything we've talked about remains confidential, and thanks again – I've really enjoyed our conversation today."

Option 2: Client is choosing their coach by meeting with shortlisted coaches (usually a maximum of three) for chemistry meetings.

Again, in this scenario we need to give the client time to reflect and signpost what happens next – and we also need to make it "okay" for them to choose someone else. There should be no overt "choose me, please" – just active encouragement to explore different styles and choose a coach that feels like a good fit.

This is about matching client needs to a coaching style and potential for partnership.

E.g. "Thanks so much for your time today; I've really enjoyed our conversation and getting a sense of what you'd like to work on. Hopefully this chat has given you a flavour of how our conversations might feel if we were to work together.

"It's really important for you to experience different coaches' styles, and to feel what it might be like to work with each one. As you know, coaching is a partnership and it's essential that you have confidence in your partner and what you could achieve together. I feel confident that we could work well together and do some great work around xyz." **(Only say this if you mean it – see next page!)**

(If we don't make a statement about our feelings ("I feel confident...") clients may assume that we're suggesting they meet other coaches because we don't feel we can work with them – rather than acting ethically/in line with good practice.)

Now, your **next steps** need careful framing to make sure that you model sensitivity, integrity and adequately signpost the practical next stage (contracting).

E.g. "Once you've met all of the coaches, it's for you to decide who you'd like to partner with. Coaches work to an ethical code, which means that we want what's best for you and will fully respect your choice of partner.

"When you've decided who you'd like to work with, speak to (coaching co-ordinator/the coaches) and arrange a set-up meeting with your chosen coach. This is where you'll pin down the specifics around what you want to achieve and how we'll work together.

"Rest assured that everything we've talked about remains confidential."

And finally – now for the final ethical "goodbye" line.

Quick Tip-in-Practice: Remember – no manipulation or subtle "pick me" – such as "I hope we can work together". This isn't ethical.

"I hope coaching helps you achieve (xyz) and that you enjoy a really powerful and productive coaching relationship with whichever coach you choose."

Develop your OWN version of the "goodbye" line.

What if I feel we can't work together or I'm not equipped to support them?

Be honest: if you genuinely feel that the client would be better served by another coach, then signpost them – gently – through your feedback and phrasing. If they're looking for specific inputs/experience then this is easy:

E.g. "While I have some experience of xyz, it's not my main area of focus; you might want to see if there are other more specialist coaches who could help you."

If you felt a lack of connection then test this out by asking the client how they experienced the flow/how they felt within the conversation; explore your (unspoken) observations and – if calibrated by the client – encourage them to test out how it feels with one or two other coaches. It's helpful to position this as standard practice; often clients will become more comfortable as they experience more coaches through chemistry meetings.

> **Remember**: it could simply be a difference in communication preferences which – as a coach – you can adapt to. Challenge yourself and test your observations.

At a glance – "How do I run a chemistry meeting?"

- Maximum 45 minutes – in-person, via video call or via phone.
- Surround the conversation with a shield of confidentiality.
- It's not a sell – it's a practical demonstration of your coaching style/flavour. Client considerations: 4/5 Cs.
- Typical structure:
    - **Intro**: Rapport-building, purpose, check timings, confidentiality
    - **Main body**: Facilitate around two base questions:
        - What's your previous experience of working with a coach?
        - What's prompted you to look for a coach right now?
    - **Close**:
        - Summary of what's been covered – any questions?
        - Feedback, thanks and signpost next steps
        - Ethical "goodbye" line and restate confidentiality
- Craft your own versions of the base questions and closing/"goodbye" line. Your language must feel authentic to you.

Contracting is...

... the start of our journey together.

Establishing the **partnership**, setting the **destination** – and agreeing how we'll know when we've arrived.

As well as sorting out all the **practical stuff** we'll need on the journey.

CHAPTER 8
Contracting – the journey begins

Coaches frequently ask:

> **What do I need to cover in a contracting meeting?**

This is often accompanied by supplementary questions such as:

- How long should I allow for a contracting meeting?
- Who should attend?
- What form does it take? Is it a written contract?

Contracting is a practice that everyone agrees is super important. Professional bodies advocate effective contracting and well-respected coaching authors position it as the "single most important conversation within the coaching relationship". And yet there's scarce information available on what's actually covered within that conversation.

Why is this? Well, firstly, contracting within coaching is relatively new; it's only in the last 10 to 15 years that there has been any focused recognition of its role and importance and any rigour placed around contracting in practice. Secondly, it's practice based; all coaches will develop their own way of undertaking the contracting conversation. As such, there's no definitive roadmap, framework or "right/wrong" way of doing it. But there *are* agreed principles which can help shape our approach.

My intention in this chapter is to explore the what, why, who, when and how of contracting, and to share some practical tips and "How to's" – all of which have been tried and tested through my own practice and through the work of my coach-students and supervisees.

Let's start by taking a moment to clarify what exactly is meant by the term "contracting", why it's important and where it sits within the coaching assignment.

Contracting – definition, role and purpose

The term "contracting" in a coaching context means agreeing how the partnership will work (roles and responsibilities), what you'll be working on (scope and goal) and how you'll both recognise when you've achieved it (measures/KPIs).

> **Quick Tip-in-Practice:** Contracting is coach jargon and the word itself may sound overly formal. I tend to use more everyday language when referring to the contracting conversation; some of my favourites include: "set-up" or "baseline" or "kick-off" meeting.

Whichever label you choose, it serves the same purpose: it's an explicit agreement from which the coaching relationship can move forward and operate.

All coaching relationships will benefit from the presence of an explicit agreement of principles and practicalities, whether it's a formal coaching assignment – contracted with an external or internal coach – or an informal line-manager coaching arrangement.

Why is contracting important?

Here are some authored positions on the role and importance of contracting:

- Peter Hill identifies that "As in most relationships, participants in coaching relationships tend to make implicit, critical assumptions about the relationship: about its purpose, about roles and responsibilities, about coaching methods and about the other party's willingness. *When the assumptions aren't aligned, trouble can ensue in the partnership."* Concepts for Coaching (Hill, 2004)

- Contracting for a formal partnership is a way to make these assumptions explicit. *"By contracting we mean reaching an explicit operating agreement that provides structure, guidance and alignment for both parties for the duration of the partnership – in essence, the ground rules."*

- Anne Scoular in *Business Coaching* (Scoular, 2011) includes it in her "Big Five" basic skills for business coaching; she maintains that *"When something goes wrong in coaching, 99% of the time it was a failure in the initial contracting."*

- In *Adaptive Coaching* (Bacon & Voss, 2012) the authors position it as *"expectation setting"* without which the coach risks *"providing the wrong kind of coaching, on the wrong issues, at the wrong time... and never building the kind of trust and confidence essential in a coaching relationship."*

So the message here is clear:

Contracting is a crucial conversation – it provides the partnership with agreed terms of reference from which we can deliver and hold each other accountable.

Essentially, through contracting, we're preparing for the journey. We're identifying the client's destination and key landmarks, agreeing our individual roles and responsibilities and checking that we have the resources we need.

At the same time, we're dealing with some of the practical stuff – such as how and when we travel.

Contracting – where does it fit and who's involved?

The contracting meeting is the first in the coaching assignment: you've been selected (via chemistry) as the coach for this assignment, and the contracting conversation is the beginning of the partnership and its journey.

Mid-point review

Try to schedule the contracting meeting as soon as practically possible after you've been selected as a coach. This is so you can capture the momentum and motivation gained from the chemistry.

Make it clear to the client that this first scheduled meeting in the series has a specific (set-up) purpose to provide the partnership with a solid platform from which to work together.

> **Quick Tip-in-Practice:**
> Always separate the contracting meeting from any coaching.
> It's a standalone session with a specific purpose.

We need the client to distinctly remember this session – the tone, content and characteristics – as the discussion we had at the beginning of the relationship, where we pinned down what we're working on and how we're going to work together. Our base camp conversation.

Creating the set-up as a standalone meeting helps to differentiate the conversation in the client's memory and improves the chances of recall and recognition. This is important as we may need to pull back to some of the specifics later on in the assignment.

> E.g. "Do you remember when we started this journey, we agreed how we'd..."

Contracting – the "bungee-rope conversation"

Think of the contracting meeting as your bungee base camp. Providing the rope is strong and well-anchored we can travel great distances at speed, confident that the strength of the anchor plates – combined with the power of our momentum – will always bring us back to base camp.

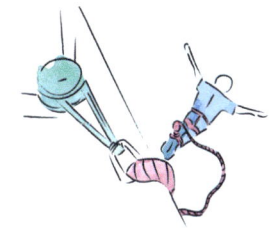

Timing and scheduling

It's useful to get your first coaching session in the diary as soon after contracting as possible; having set up the partnership, the client will be keen to start the journey. And we need to leverage the positive momentum created from the set-up.

> **Quick Tip-in-Practice:** If – for logistical reasons (long journey/client availability) – you absolutely need to cover contracting and deliver your first coaching session in a "double session/single visit", make sure that the two sessions are delineated and have space between them, however short. You can do this by saying something like, "Let's take a comfort break… see you back in 10."

Don't skimp on the time allowed for contracting (typically 60 to 90 minutes depending on context, goals and how many parties are involved in the conversation). If your coaching sessions are 60 to 90 minutes long too, you'll need to schedule a good chunk of time (between two and a half and three hours) to cover both effectively.

Who needs to be involved?

The nature of the contracting conversation will depend on whether it's a two or three-party arrangement. When coaching is requested by the client and it's exclusively their agenda, it can be entirely appropriate for contracting to involve just the coach and the client (i.e. two-way contracting).

If the coaching has been organised for the client – at someone else's request or suggestion – then it may be helpful to involve other parties in the contracting. Three-way contracting typically involves the coach, client and line manager or sponsor; typically, the third party is present for some parts of the conversation (see Key Ingredients section) and then leaves the coach and client to finish up.

Involving the line manager or sponsor in the contracting provides an opportunity for all parties to input and achieve clarity on expectations and the roles they'll play in supporting the coaching assignment.

> **Quick Tip-in-Practice:** If the coaching has been requested by someone other than the client, then it's really helpful to get that person involved in the contracting conversation. It helps avoid back-briefing situations and sub-agendas, which could undermine trust within the coaching relationship.

Often formal coaching assignments will begin with triad (three-way) contracting and end with triad closing; this enables the key stakeholders to set expectations and then review progress against the agreed aims. Building it in as standard practice encourages trust and openness and supports the identification of robust and relevant goals and measures.

What form does it take? Is it a written contract?

No, it's usually a conversation that may be documented afterwards.

Contracting is NOT necessarily about signing a written document or agreeing commercial terms and fees; good practice ensures that any commercial arrangements are taken care of BEFORE contracting* – via the sponsor or relevant party – so that the client and coach are free to focus on getting underway.

Ideally, commercial arrangements (indicative fees/typical assignment package etc) would be determined BEFORE a chemistry meeting, so that the client isn't meeting anyone for chemistry that doesn't meet the procurement criteria/budget.

> **Contracting isn't about what's written down.** It's the psychological contract between coach and client – the relationship, how you'll work together – and the assignment scope/mission.

As such, the coach and client might agree that a written summary would be shared between them. Some organisations use templates for the contracting conversation to ensure that the content is captured consistently and the agreed outcomes, measures and practical arrangements are accurately recorded.

Whatever method you use for capturing what's been discussed at the contracting/set-up meeting, it's important to use a system that works well for you, fulfils ethical and legal requirements and which fully meets the needs of your client base.

> **Quick Tip-in-Practice:** My favoured approach is to encourage the client to capture their own record of the assignment goals and measures/KPIs.
> I then send a summary through (from my notes) for cross-checking.

You'll inevitably need to refer back to the contracting conversation and what's been agreed.

Most coaches-in-practice will document these items for their own use via Coaching Plans (or similar) and may send an email summary of what's been agreed to the client afterwards.

> **Robust contracting + good notetaking = strong foundation.**
>
> This ensures that the bungee rope is firmly anchored and we can return to base camp quickly and easily when needed.

What to cover – key ingredients

So, back to the question:

> **What do I need to cover in a contracting meeting?**

While every set-up conversation will run differently (because it's a two-way conversation and you can't script the other person) they all need to cover the same elements. Essentially this means explicit discussion – and agreement – around the:

- relationship – who's involved and how we work together
- purpose – what we work on and what we want to achieve
- practicalities – when, where and how we meet.

And around all of these we need to wrap the all-important:

- ethics and safety factors.

Over the past 20 years I've identified the following list of key ingredients that I regard as essential. If we miss any of these ingredients out, we can encounter issues later on.

List of key ingredients

1. Set the scene and purpose of meeting. (If you haven't already met for a chemistry meeting, you'll also need to cover "what coaching is/isn't" to ensure alignment of expectations and that coaching is the right choice.)
2. Relationship – trust, openness, commitment to partnership
3. Roles and responsibilities within the assignment (including other parties e.g. if three- or four-way contracting)
4. Reporting back (into sponsor/line manager) – how, when, who
5. Purpose – goals, outcomes and measurement (what's our current baseline and how will we know when we've got there)
6. Structure – number of sessions or hours, frequency, timescales
7. Feedback and review – style, challenge, progress, termination
8. Logistics – location, method, cancellation arrangements
9. Communication – methods, follow-through, interim contact, invitations
10. Code of conduct – ethics and safety factors = 4 Cs

Each of the 10 elements has a specific role to play in the contracting conversation. We'll examine the running order – and how you might cover the points – shortly.

1. Set the scene (purpose of meeting) – The coach will take the lead in facilitating this conversation. We know what needs to be covered and we've travelled this road before. Whether it's two-, three- or even four-way contracting, setting out the purpose of the set-up meeting – and what you're looking to achieve from it – is key.

If you haven't met the client before or undertaken a chemistry meeting then it's super-important to check and calibrate their understanding and expectations of coaching before you set off. Use the calibration question:

> **Q1. What's your previous experience of working with a coach?**

2. Relationship – It's always useful to facilitate some discussion around the relationship itself; refer to the "partnership" and "working together", and highlight the importance of openness and candour. Asking *"What will help you get the best from this partnership?"* and encouraging the client to describe what a good partnership looks and feels like can work really well.

3. Roles and responsibilities – It's important to facilitate discussion around individual roles and responsibilities within the partnership – even more important if you have multiple stakeholders present for the contracting. Each person needs to examine and articulate their role and responsibilities in the context of the assignment.

E.g. Coach's role is both macro (1) and micro (2): *"My role as coach is to..."* 1. Ensure that the destination is clear, we have what we need for the journey and we maintain momentum and stay on track. 2. Help explore and challenge your thinking within sessions, uncover new insights and perspectives etc.

💡 **Quick Tip-in-Practice:** Develop your own version of "My role as a coach is to..." and include both macro and micro elements.

Invite the client to explain how they see their role. The client's role and responsibilities will typically include: being open and candid, committing time and energy to the sessions and follow-through actions, being on time and in the right headspace for coaching sessions, and giving feedback to the coach.

The roles and responsibilities of other stakeholders/parties to the contracting will vary. If a line manager is involved, then their primary role will be to support the client – enabling time for the coaching sessions and subsequent actions – and being available to discuss and take action on any issues or potential obstacles to progress. Again, other stakeholders (sponsors or HR/L&D/OD professionals) may describe their role as supportive. They're likely to be less involved with client actions and more focused on supporting the wider coaching activity/macro assignment and ensuring its value to the client.

4. Reporting back – It's absolutely essential to cover this point explicitly, particularly in three- or four-way contracting. Whose responsibility will it be to update the line manager, sponsor or organisation on progress?

The client should *always* be the one to update other stakeholders on their progress. I always make it explicit within three or four-way contracting that any updates on progress will come from the client, not from me.

The only information that a coach might share would be related to the macro assignment, e.g. "We've completed four out of six scheduled sessions."

> **Quick Tip-in-Practice:** Ensure that the topic of reporting back is covered while the other parties are present. That way, you can use "the bungee rope" if they ask you for a progress update. "Remember our set up... we agreed that all updates would come from x".

In conversation this point can often fit seamlessly with Confidentiality. See Point 10.

5. Purpose – goals, outcomes and measurement – This point needs to be covered really thoroughly as we'll facilitate discussion around the purpose of the coaching – what prompted the request – and current "Reality" or landscape. Through good questioning and drill-down, we'll help the client to identify their starting point (current behaviours, how it's impacting) and some baseline measures. (Use scaling: *"On a scale of 1-10 how well do you do that now...?"* or frequency-based indicators: *"How often do you do that now?"*)

Then we'll help the client identify where they want to get to (their Goal), e.g. *"Where would you like to be (in relation to baseline); what do you want to achieve?"* and pin down specific measures around *"How will we know when we've got there?"*

Identification of goals and measures needs focused time and drill-down questioning; calibrate the current state/baseline by inviting inputs from other parties (if present) or using evidence-based questions with the client. E.g. *"What evidence do you have of xyz? How do you know that to be true?"* or using alternative-perspective questions, e.g. *"If I were to ask your colleagues about that, what would they tell me?"* You'll be regularly reviewing progress throughout the assignment so you need specifics to pull back to e.g. *"When we started, I did that once a month, and now I'm doing it four or five times a week."*

> Using scaling (1-10) or frequency-based indicators helps the client see and feel progress. Pinning down measures is motivational and supports the momentum of the assignment.

It's important to keep the discussion focused on the specific areas to be worked on and the indicators (baseline vs "to be achieved") as this helps to shape the scope and structure of the coaching assignment. (If not already pre-determined – see Point 6.)

6. Structure – The structure and goals for any assignment are co-dependent; the goal needs to be achievable within the number of sessions or contact time, and, conversely, the coaching hours need to be sufficient to achieve the desired outcomes. If the structure of the assignment is pre-determined by organisational norms or procurement (i.e. an agreed standard format of sessions/hours) then it's simply a case of matching the size/scope of the goal to the hours allocated.

Typically (more on this word shortly!) an assignment (or procured package) consists of a certain number of sessions/hours, e.g. "6x 60/90-minute sessions" or a "total of 12 hours". It's our role to ensure that we allocate time to contracting and closing; if three-way contracting has been initiated at the beginning, allow time for three-way closing at the end.

> **Quick Tip-in-Practice:** If the number of sessions or hours hasn't been defined in advance, or if you're unsure how many might be needed, use the magic all-purpose contracting word **"typically"**.
> E.g. "Typically, we'll have four to six meetings of 60/90 mins each..."
> This gives you a base position + some flexibility within the assignment.

The frequency of sessions will vary; sometimes they'll be dependent on client actions and any fixed/specific dates (e.g. the client is going to try out xyz at a quarterly meeting, speak at a conference or is going for an interview on a specific date). There may also be hard deadlines for the assignment which, again, will influence frequency.

But the general rule of thumb is that the scope of the goal and the size of the actions will shape the frequency of meetings; typically (there's that word again!) the discussion around goals and measures (Point 5) will give you sufficient feel for the scope and expectations so that you can determine an appropriate pattern and frequency.

> **Quick Tip-in-Practice:** Avoid diarising the whole sequence in advance as this can impact on momentum and the amount of stretch in the actions. Schedule one session ahead and – when discussing time/scheduling – use the magic all-purpose contracting word **"typically"**.
> "Typically, we'd meet every four to five weeks unless there are specific reasons for us to meet earlier or later."

By framing the frequency in this way, it gives the client a sense of the timescale and how long the journey is likely to take. As above, if there are "hard deadlines", such as starting a new job or going for an interview, then the overall timescale is fixed. Either way, having an overall feel for the timescale helps remind the client of their role in driving progress; meetings will be linked to the actions they take – big steps usually mean a longer gap between sessions – and models the dynamic of the assignment.

> **Assignments vary in shape and size**; the fleet of boats at our disposal ranges from a two-man kayak to an ocean-going yacht.
> Match the choice of vessel to the needs of the journey.

7. Feedback and review – It's important to explain you'll be regularly reviewing progress and asking for feedback throughout the journey, and discuss how important this ongoing two-way dialogue is to the success of the partnership. As a coach, you need to know what works – and what doesn't – for the client, and what degree of challenge they want/have experienced in the session. But careful framing and phrasing are key.

> **Quick Tip-in-Practice:** Clients can be reluctant to give feedback during the assignment for fear of damaging the relationship. **Don't use the "f" (feedback) word**.
> "So, thinking about the way we've worked today, what was useful/helpful?" and then dig down…"What specifically made it helpful for you?"

Within this section it's an opportunity to raise the issue of terminating the assignment (although we'd NEVER use this word!). What if it's not working? What if there's no progress or the relationship is scratchy or non-productive? The phrase "an appropriate way forward" is another super-useful contracting phrase; it sits up there with "typically"!

> **Quick Tip-in-Practice:** Combine review and signpost "termination". E.g. "As well as reviewing progress against your goals, we'll regularly check in on how we're working together, including a structured review at the mid-point. If either of us feels that we're not achieving what we'd hoped, then we'll discuss it and agree an **appropriate way forward**, which may include pausing or ending the coaching."

8. Logistics – This point covers the practicalities associated with where and how you meet – what options you have available or are prepared to consider. Find out whether your client wants to meet at work or off-site, in-person or online/by phone – or a combination of these things. Note that this may be influenced by the terms of the procurement/package agreed. If you're using virtual meetings, find out whether your client has a preference for a specific platform.

It's also important to understand which days and times work best for your client. Explore working patterns such as office days, non-working days, busy times of the month, plus any care-related commitments which might impact on availability.

You also need to discuss what will happen if either of you needs to cancel a scheduled session and rearrange. If you have travel arrangements to consider (for in-person meetings) then agree how much notice is needed to avoid cost and time implications.

9. Communication – It's really helpful to discuss with the client how you'll communicate after and in between the sessions and who will do what. As well as client contact details it's useful to know their preferred method of communication. Agree any follow-through actions (confirmation of actions or session notes and invitations to next meeting) and decide who will routinely take responsibility for these actions.

What degree of contact are you prepared and able to support in between sessions? Are you offering a 24/7 coach hotline? While we want to support and be accessible we need to manage client expectations – it's a fine balance.

> **Quick Tip-in-Practice:** Typically, I find that this approach works well: "If anything urgent crops up that you want to discuss just drop me an email and we'll arrange a call."

10. Code of Conduct = ethics and safety factors – the 4 Cs of Contracting

We need to ensure that safety factors are in place and that we can articulate our standards and the ethics (rules) that surround our coaching practice. All of the coaching membership organisations have a requirement for coaches to make explicit reference to their Code of Conduct (or Code of Ethics) when meeting with the client, and to ensure that a copy of the relevant code is made available to the client. Irrespective of which code you're working to, they all cover similar content – some of which needs to be explained and specifically verbalised – during the set-up meeting.

I call these elements the 4 Cs of Contracting (for no reason other than they all start with the letter "C").

- **Code of Conduct/Ethics** – Explain that you work to a code, and which one it is. Explain how the client can access a copy of the code.

- **Confidentiality** – As explained previously, the "shield of confidentiality" needs to be made explicit. Confirm that all conversations are confidential, any notes taken will be stored securely and in accordance with relevant data protection legislation and the conditions under which information might be shared.

- **Competence** – It's important to emphasise boundaries of experience/where you're qualified or equipped to go. Coaching is not counselling.

- **Conflict of interest** – This specific item of the codes is super important, particularly if you're coaching within an organisation. By contracting explicitly around how you'll deal with any potential conflicts of interest, it ensures that they can be surfaced and handled effectively. Most common conflicts of interest are typically around being asked to coach someone within the client's direct managerial relationship, or participating in career activity that may be related to the client, e.g. the coach may be asked to support selection/development activities or interviews in which the client is involved.

> **Quick Tip-in-Practice:** The 4 Cs of Contracting are my shorthand to help remember which code elements need to be explicitly covered in contracting. You'll find sample one-liners on how to cover these within the Style section which follows. Build your own versions of these one-liners and practise to achieve fluency.

Okay, so that looks like a fairly standard list of 10 themes you'd expect to cover in a set-up meeting. But, of course, this is a conversation where you're facilitating discussion around each of these elements.

> Don't think of it as a list of items to be covered; like any list of ingredients, the order in which they're added and the stage of the cooking is crucial – it often determines the success of the dish. Some ingredients are put in at the beginning, others are sprinkled in as they're needed.

Structure – the "burger and the bun"

I often use the analogy of the burger and the bun when describing the structure of the contracting conversation. Essentially:

- The burger is the "meat" or main purpose of the coaching assignment. We need to explore the goals; our starting point (or baseline); and clear (scaled) measures/indicators of how we'll know when we've achieved it. All of this will take up a large part of the conversation. Typically, a good burger will take around 40–50% of the time, e.g. 30 to 40 minutes.

- The two parts of the bun – the top and bottom – represent the other elements to be covered which support and contain the "burger". Some base items, such as confidentiality, will have fixed positions (in this case, at the beginning, or in the top part of the bun). Other elements will form a part of the "ending" (the bun base), e.g. logistics, date for next meeting etc.

- Other filling elements will be sprinkled in as and when the opportunity arises.

- And not all items are equal.

> Make sure you're delivering a good, solid quarter pounder, not a thin slice of salami.
> Quality time needs to be spent drilling down around the goal and measures – otherwise you can't recognise progress.

Chapter 8 | Contracting – the journey begins

Here's a typical contracting structure of the 10 items, applying a burger and bun approach.

Key: The items in blue are those typically covered in three- or four-way contracting meetings. We've identified each item.

1. Set the scene
10. Code + Confidentiality
2. Relationship: candid and open
10. Competence – boundaries

3. Roles and responsibilities
4. Reporting back (into organisation/line manager)

5. Purpose – context/background – drivers/focus areas/priorities
Baseline – current indicators/measures
Goal: Where we want to get to – what will that look like/scores/indicators?
6. Structure – no. of sessions/hours/frequency (link to goal)

7. Feedback and review progress
7. Rights to terminate (for all parties)
10. Conflicts of interest

8. Logistics – when (working patterns), where (location and mode), cancellation arrangements
9. Communication – how (method), follow-through – agree date for first coaching session

Quick Tip-in-Practice: Create your own "map" of what needs to be covered. Keep it fluid and agile so that you can adapt to the client responses; keep it visual so that you can see at a glance where you need to go next.

The all-important "how" of contracting

In my view, **what** is covered and **how** we cover it are of equal importance.

Both need to be covered fluently, confidently and in our own style to set up the partnership for a successful journey. That means knowing our destination, what roles we'll play in achieving it and having clear expectations of each other.

> If we cover the wrong things – or miss some out – we add risk to the assignment and to the relationship.
> If we cover the right elements in the "wrong" way we add risk to the underpinning trust and openness within the relationship.

So we must balance the needs of the assignment (managing the underpinning macro process and practicalities) with the needs of the relationship. Don't let your desire to cover all of the "right" things in contracting overtake the need to model partnership – and a coaching style to guide our client's journey.

> The journey is as important as the destination; given the right climate and support, our client will gain valuable by-products from their experience of travelling with us.
> Coaching develops self-coaching; we hope our clients develop additional insights, self-awareness, confidence and tools/techniques to self-challenge and self-coach when we're not around and once the journey ends.

As coaches, we're likely to be the more experienced travellers: we've been with clients on similar journeys before so it's appropriate that we're facilitating the contracting elements. We need to make sure we've packed everything we're going to need for the journey and anticipated any challenges.

We need to model fluency and confidence in the set-up; as the experienced traveller it's important that we look as if we know what we're doing, and that our style models partnership and confidence. That will inspire confidence and buy-in from our client.

But – and here's the thing – we face a double challenge.

> Contracting only happens once per assignment.
> So we naturally have less experience of running these conversations and less opportunity to practise and hone our fluency.
> Preparation is key.

Style – key principles

The coach will take the lead in facilitating this conversation – after all, we know what needs to be covered. There are some aspects that require input, such as the 4 Cs of Contracting, as they need to be explicitly stated. So this set-up conversation will have a slightly different feel to it – and this helps to differentiate it in the client's memory. Remember: the bungee rope can always spring back to refer to this meeting.

- **High-energy!** This is the start of your journey together – convey energy and enthusiasm in your phrases, tone and body language, e.g. *"I'm really looking forward to working with you... it's great to get started!"*

- **Two-way conversation**: Facilitate each point using questions to invite input from the client (and sponsor if present). Don't be tempted to work through your "list" – it won't set the right tone for your partnership.

- **Adult–Adult**: As above, it may be tempting to slip into "tell" mode (almost like you're the parent) but we need to keep this conversation in adult–adult mode. Asking the client for their inputs – *"What are your thoughts around...? What do you see as..."* – will ensure you access the thinking (adult) state.

- **Create a mind map/crib sheet**: Create a fluid "map" of the items you need to cover, together with prompt questions or key points. This will help you remember what needs to be covered and to move fluently around the conversation without it feeling rigid. Sprinkle the points as and when the opportunity arises.

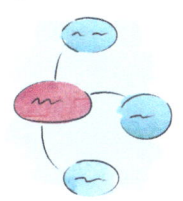

- **Create your own one-liner explanations** for each of the 4 Cs of Contracting and cover each one individually (as a set they'll feel like a block of concrete).

    o Code of Conduct/Ethics – e.g. *"As a coach I work to a recognised Code of Ethics which sets out the standards for good practice; I'm going to signpost relevant elements of the code during this conversation – a copy of the code is available to you on request."*

    o Confidentiality – e.g. *"Everything we discuss is confidential and any notes that I take will be stored securely in accordance with (legislation). I won't be sharing details with anyone else unless there is a threat to your safety or a legal requirement for me to do so."*

    o Competence – e.g. *"I'm not going to go anywhere I'm not trained or equipped to go; I'm a coach – not a therapist or counsellor – and our conversations will stay within a coaching remit."*

    o Conflict of interest – e.g. *"If either of us becomes aware of any potential for a conflict of interest, we'll discuss it and agree an appropriate way forward."*

- **Develop your own versions** of the 4 Cs – and **practise them out loud**.

Troubleshooting the set-up – some frequently asked questions

What if I forget something?

Firstly, only you will know that you've missed something; you're the seasoned traveller – the client won't know as they haven't undertaken this journey before.

Secondly, when did you notice? If you noticed because the omission caused an issue later in the assignment then lean into it; open up a discussion with the client to clarify what's causing the issue and how it's impacting and then agree an appropriate way forward. If, on the other hand, you became aware of the missing item because your record-keeping highlighted the omission then raise it at the next session – without highlighting that it was missed!

> *"Just to recap: last time we discussed specifically how we'd work together and what we're aiming to achieve. We talked about x and y; at this point it's also worth mentioning z, which..."*

Quick Tip-in-Practice: Good record-keeping helps ensure that you cover all of the contracting items on your "map" or cribsheet. Adding a checklist to your Coaching Plan template helps highlight omissions and acts as a record of what was covered and agreed with each client.

I was talking for 80% of the time – is that normal for contracting?

No. It sounds like you fell into the trap of *telling* or inputting the points, instead of dialling up the ask and facilitating a two-way discussion. While contracting does have some specific coach inputs (e.g. the 4 Cs) and there will be more (invisible) guidance from the coach because we know what we need to cover, you should still achieve a 50/50 balance. Remember: the goal and measures need significant client input (to ensure a quarter pounder) so this often rebalances the conversation.

Having explored the client's baseline and goal we automatically started exploring potential strategies to fix the gap

This happens when a coach forgets that they're contracting and starts to coach; it's the age-old "helping" or "need-to-fix" gene kicking in. When we're exploring the issue and identifying the client baseline we're in the Reality phase of the GROW model. Then we move to Goal. If you're starting to explore strategies to solve it then you've fallen into Options phase, which isn't part of the set-up.

Quick Tip-in-Practice: Use the summary to bring the conversation back on track.
E.g. "We've talked about where you are currently and where you want to get to through coaching. Now let's look at some of the practicalities around helping you get there..."

Recapping – at a glance

> ## What do I need to cover in a contracting meeting?

- Schedule a standalone session – it needs to feel different. It's useful to think of a bungee rope that can always return or refer back to this meeting.
- Involve other parties (three/four-way contracting as appropriate).
- Remember what is covered is of equal importance to how we cover it – it should feel like a dialogue between two adults.
- Consider the structure (burger & bun!). Don't skimp on the burger – make it a quarter pounder.
- Typical structure of a session lasting 60 to 90 minutes:
    - **Bun/Above the burger:**
        - Set the scene + some of 4 Cs Code + relationship
        - Roles and responsibilities and reporting back
    - **Burger: Where are we now/where do we want to get to/how will we know when we've got there?**
        - Purpose: drivers/context + baseline (current position)
        - Goal and measures (scaling and frequency indicators)
    - **Bun/Below the burger:**
        - Feedback and review plus right to terminate
        - Logistics + communication
        - Next steps
- Craft your own versions of the 4 Cs one liners and practise until fluent.
- The contracting conversation needs to be fluent, but... it's the conversation we do least often. Create a map or cribsheet to support consistency and fluency.

⚠️ This conversation should feel energising. We need to project the excitement that the seasoned traveller feels as the journey begins! Just remember to hold the conversation to R (Reality) and G (Goals); don't fall into O (Options)! That's for your first coaching conversation!

Staying on course...

... keeping the wind in our sails and the tiller steady.

Holding true to the North Star – **driving forward** with strong engines when the sails are empty or the currents are pulling us back.

CHAPTER 9
Maintaining course and momentum

Most coaches have encountered slowdown within an assignment, which is why one of the most asked questions and most requested discussion topics is:

> **The assignment is losing momentum... what can I do?**

Journeys usually begin with huge excitement, energy and motivation. They feel like the start of something new. An adventure. But, once we're underway, the rhythm of the travel normalises the energy. The focus can drop and all of our time is spent keeping the travellers entertained and effectively trying to shorten the journey.

Inevitably, the chorus of "Are we there yet?" and "How much further?" starts to pierce the conversation until – at last – the destination is within countdown distance and focus shifts from the journey to the arrival at our destination.

To journey is to arrive

The difference in a coaching context is that – of course – it's not *just* about the destination. Coaching isn't about travelling a straight line from A to B via the quickest route; we're not flying a commercial airline and choosing the fastest route with shortest airport transfers. The journey is as important as the destination.

> We're on twin journeys: towards a destination (the outcomes of the coaching sessions) *and* within the coaching relationship itself. How we travel together and the insights gained throughout the assignment will have an influence on the level of the client's final achievement.

You might have noticed that I reference sailing rather than flying. That's because when sailing we have more in-the-moment control. Tack a little to the left and let's catch the breeze and fill the sails. If there's no wind, we can start the engine. And we'll ride the energy of the waves, we'll anticipate where the currents and risks are and navigate around them. Together.

We might take unplanned detours, but our compass is set to our North Star and we'll always get back on course. And we'll harness the forces of nature and take every bit of learning from our journey.

> Our role as a coach is to check the wind speed and direction, anticipate risks to progress, and know when and how to start the engine.

Losing momentum – what's going on?

So the coaching journey's off to a flying start. Our contracting meeting generated some really clear outcomes and we've agreed how to get best value from the partnership. Energy, commitment and motivation were visibly high.

And that continued through the first and second subsequent coaching conversations; the client was focused and determined and followed through on all the identified actions. Communication was good and responses were instant. And then something shifted.

The third session was rescheduled twice by the client. When you did meet there was less energy in the room, fewer new insights from the client, and there was noticeably less stretch in the identified actions which came out of the conversation. And the date for the next session wasn't pinned down. It felt different. It *was* different.

As a coach you had to work harder. The voice in your head is asking "What's happening here? Where's the energy? What's changed? What am I doing wrong?" as your confidence comes under fire. We've all been there. The feeling that a coaching assignment is losing momentum or is not moving forward as you'd anticipated.

The short answer is:

> **You're not doing anything "wrong".**
> The journey – and the relationship – will go through different phases.
> You're simply noticing indicators of a different phase.

The most important thing to recognise is that this is normal. It happens in most journeys – and relationships – and in lots of coaching assignments.

> **Quick Tip-in-Practice:** Don't hit the panic button and internalise or blame yourself or the client.
> Step out and look at the macro assignment objectively.
> We need to find out what's going on so we can address it, restart the engine and get back on track.

Let's start with these three steps:

1. Symptoms – What symptoms of delay/loss of momentum are you noticing?

- List all of your noticings (observations) from the beginning of assignment to the current point; refer to your coaching notes. Include observations at macro (assignment) and micro (session) level.

- Be factual. How are sessions scheduled? What's the frequency? Communication and response times from the client? What changes have you noticed? If you were to scale the client energy, openness and commitment within the sessions, how would they rate? How would you compare Contracting vs Session 1 vs Session 2, etc?

2. Test assumptions and evidence – What assumptions are you making?

- Comparisons – As well as comparing early client behaviour and patterns with the latest behaviour, what other comparisons are you making? Are you comparing the patterns in this assignment with other assignments?

- If so, how valid is that comparison? What are the similarities/differences in:
    o Client topics – complexity/challenges/dependencies/risks
    o Client – personality traits/motivation for coaching/openness energy levels
    o Client operating environment – pressures/resources/priorities/support

3. Drag or drift? – What's the cause?

Having determined that this assignment IS slowing down, consider what factors are impacting on the momentum. Over the years as I've explored this issue, I've identified that various factors may be responsible. I've called them "drag" and "drift", and either – or both – of these may contribute to a loss of traction.

Drag factors involve anything that actively slows down progress, and act as a brake on forward progress and momentum. This may include intrinsic elements (client motivation, feelings, beliefs) or extrinsic factors (workload/climate/complexity of actions).

   o **Drag factors are usually person-centred**. Both conscious and unconscious influences may act as drag factors.

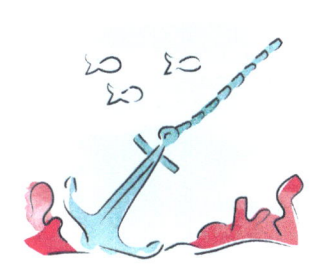

Drift factors are things which delay, influence or impact on the overall structure of the assignment. Factors which create a feeling that the assignment is freewheeling or drifting, without clear line of sight to a destination, timescale or anchor point.

   o **Drift is usually process-related**. It's often related to the management of the macro assignment and the underpinning communication and scheduling processes.

⚠ Drift factors can impact and enhance drag factors – and vice versa. Drag factors may be internal or external to the client, creating currents that pull against progress.

What can affect momentum – drift factors

Let's start with "drift". It's usually easy to spot and fairly straightforward to fix/get the engine restarted.

Often a lack of momentum, or a feeling that the coaching assignment is stuck or losing pace, is due to points of weakness in the assignment structure and/or the underpinning processes.

As the coach – and the more experienced traveller – it's our responsibility to manage these underpinning processes and ensure our practices are robust and effective, and that the partnership is working productively.

Scheduling of sessions

- Consider the mechanism and influences:
  - How are sessions scheduled? In advance? Or by the client as and when they feel ready? How is scheduling linked to client actions? How often are sessions being rescheduled? What are the reasons? And what's the impact of having longer gaps between sessions?
  - How does this compare with what you agreed at contracting? When did you last review the pattern of sessions with the client?
- Monitoring and tracking scheduled sessions:
  - How are you tracking client sessions? Is your method visible and accessible/effective enough to notice timescales drifting out? Are you using a manual or an automated prompt system?
- Communications – review of method, frequency, response times:
  - If the client cancels and then promises to get in touch when they're able to, how long do you leave it before getting in touch? How do you prompt them?
  - It's important to maintain an adult–adult tone when prompting – this is a partnership of equals after all. Emphasise the impact on progress and/or refer back to what was agreed at set-up.

"Hi X, hope all well, etc. It's x weeks since we last met, and I know how keen you are to keep up the pace on (topic)/achieve (goal) by (date). I'm looking forward to hearing how you're progressing.

Currently I can offer xyz dates/times. Please let me know which of these suits or if further options are needed. Best, etc."

Quick Tip-in-Practice: Use technology! Set calendar prompts to chase. I.e. "last session with client x was # weeks/months ago" and "client committed to schedule next session by x (date)." Add to your task list so that you have visible prompts.

- Follow-through from sessions. What was agreed at contracting? (E.g. coach (or client) to send through a summary of key themes/actions.) What's in place vs what's needed?

- Coaches often fall into the trap of taking on the PA/scribe role in the relationship. Consider the purpose and timing of any session follow-through. It should be a prompt to support momentum rather than a list of client actions. (You've already captured these in your coaching notes.)

> **Quick Tip-in-Practice:** My favoured approach is to send a follow-through email to the client exactly **one week** after the session. It briefly references key themes discussed and top-level action points. **Confidentiality**: I always use shared client "code" – phrases with meanings that are specific to the client conversation – so that anyone else with access to the client email (e.g. a PA) can't decipher the detail.

"It was great to see you again last week. As per my usual practice, here's a summary of the key themes we discussed:

- Strategic vision – stakeholder "horns and halo" – chunk up comms

- Landing the brand – opportunities to dial up specifics – etc.

Thanks for the calendar invitation; I look forward to meeting again on xyz."

- Stages of relationship – different stages of the relationship often have specific characteristics which can impact on momentum. Consciously reviewing the stage of the macro assignment in the context of these typical indicators can help maintain momentum, support the relationship and avoid drift.

  - Early stages: contracting/first or second sessions – energy and motivation are high, actions are delivered and momentum is strong. Trust and relationships are beginning to establish.

  - Middle stage: momentum is often lost once the initial excitement wears off and the quick wins have been achieved. Trust is developing and the complexity of issues may increase. The pattern of sessions may change from the mid-point onwards.

  - Ending: trust is high and the end of assignment is signposted. The penultimate/final sessions may attract "endings-related" behaviour, e.g. avoidance or repetitive rescheduling. (More on this in Chapter 10.)

> ⚠️ Experience tells us that most clients will pick the "low-hanging fruit" first: in the early stages of the relationship they'll often take the quick, easy (often task-related) actions.
> Then – as confidence and trust increase – they'll start addressing and digging into the more challenging (often behavioural) areas.
> Naturally, bigger steps may mean bigger gaps between sessions.

What can affect momentum – drag factors

While drift in an assignment is relatively simple to fix (after all, we're effectively fixing points of weakness in the underpinning framework in order to generate momentum), drag factors are more complex. Drag factors can contribute to, or even cause drift.

> **Drag factors**: I define drag factors as "anything that actively slows down, creates resistance or prevents progress in the coaching assignment".
> **Drag factors are person-centred**: they can be internal or external to the client, and may be conscious or unconscious in their origin.

Having confirmed that progress and energy within a coaching assignment definitely IS slowing, it's important to try and identify where the drag is coming from. Without understanding its origins, we can't help the client devise mitigating strategies; we need to rule in or rule out each of the potential factors.

> There's no point in jumpstarting an engine which has no fuel.
> Is the tank empty? Might there be dirt in the fuel line?
> Full sails won't help a sailboat that's run aground.

Through my own coaching practice and the supervision of developing coaches I've noticed that the drag factors typically fall into a number of themes:

- 1. Goals
- 2. Motivation
- 3. Actions
- 4. Control/Influence
- 5. External factors
- 6. Feelings & beliefs

(all centred on the Client)

When facilitating the exploration of potential drag factors, it's important that we look holistically and recognise the influences of one factor on another – as well as the potential of several factors to combine and create, or contribute to, drift.

Let's first check in on what's typically covered by each of these themes:

1. Goals – To what extent is the goal itself acting as a drag factor? Are the original goals still relevant/achievable? Have priorities changed? Do goals/measures need to be tweaked?

2. Motivation – Motivation can come from within or come from external factors (pleasing others/receiving praise, etc).

- How does the level of motivation now compare with the level at the start of the journey? What's changed?

- How motivated is the client to undertake change? Is the client's motivation "towards" or "away from"? (In NLP terms, are they running TO something versus running away FROM something?) Often "away from" energy/motivation can deliver poor choices or random selection of a destination, i.e. "anywhere but here".

- What level of motivation is derived from progress vs the relationship?

3. Actions – To what extent might the actions identified/committed to by the client at each session be acting as a drag factor? These may link to motivation (above) and create drift.

- Too big? Consider the size and scale of individual actions. Are they achievable within the timescale? Are there any dependencies which are preventing the client achieving them? Do they need chunking down? If commitments are too big, your client may postpone/cancel meetings if they're not completed in time.

- Too small? Actions which feel like they're really small (baby steps) can be as much of a drag factor as actions which are too big or ambitious. Progress is less visible and may impact motivation. Actions need to contain some stretch – and we need to recognise that low-hanging fruit will be picked first. This leaves us to climb right to the top of the tree later on for the remaining fruit.

4. Control/influence – How much control or influence does the client have (or feel they have) over their actions and progress? What's directly within their control and what can they influence? Expanding awareness of what's within a client's influence and direct control – and what's outside of it – can be hugely motivational and reduce self-limiting beliefs.

5. External factors – How is the client's external environment impacting? A volatile, uncertain, complex or ambiguous (VUCA) organisational climate/conflicting priorities/ economic or resource challenges can all impact on the energy and motivation that's available to create change.

And finally, underpinning the other five themes:

6. Feelings and beliefs – It's important to explore the client's feelings and beliefs around their goals, actions, progress and what they can influence, as well as the coaching relationship and process. Feeling that it's either pointless, unachievable or not working is tantamount to dropping anchor.

> If we try and start the engine without exploring feelings and beliefs around the journey and the progress being made, we risk pulling against the force of a 200lb anchor driven deep into the seabed.

Tackling drag and drift – introducing the mid-point review

It's interesting that while most coaches recognise the importance of contracting and closing – and we're all aware that we'll regularly review progress within each session – very little attention is given to the role of a scheduled **mid-point review**.

Probably the most important tool for coaches to maintain momentum within an assignment, the mid-point review represents the ideal opportunity to review both progress and partnership. You may have noticed that we (subtly) mentioned it in contracting/set-up (see Chapter 8: Contracting, Item 7 – Feedback and Review).

> Building a mid-point review into your standard assignment structure enables you to formally check progress and investigate any drag and drift.
> It normalises the review rather than making it an exceptional feature.

Mid-point review – where does it fit in?

Typically, we'd schedule the mid-point review at the mid-point in the agreed schedule of sessions. This is determined either by session number or timescale.

For example in the series below, we'd facilitate the mid-point review either at the beginning or end of Session 3, as it's a "contracting" + "five sessions" + "close" format.

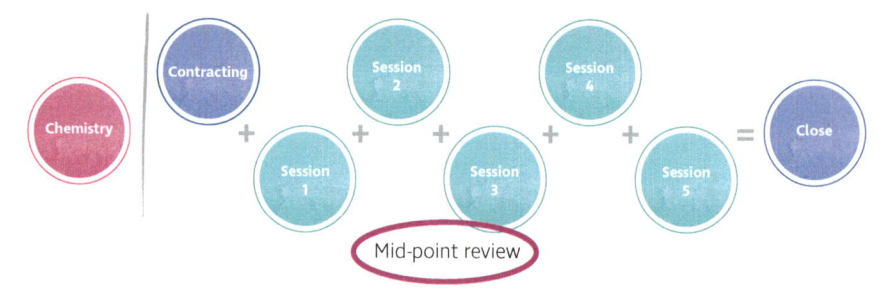

Chemistry | Contracting + Session 1 + Session 2 + Session 3 + Session 4 + Session 5 = Close

Mid-point review

Make sure that you've signposted the inclusion of a mid-point review to the client during the previous meeting, and build extra time into the next session to accommodate the mid-point. (I usually suggest adding an extra 30 minutes.)

> **Quick Tip-in-Practice:** Link the role of the mid-point to the contracting conversation. This helps to signpost that we're going to refer back to the principles agreed at our initial base camp discussion.
> **It also signposts that we're halfway through our planned schedule.**

E.g. "You'll remember that in our set-up meeting we agreed to regularly review progress and how we're working together. At our next meeting we'll review how it's working – where we started, where the challenges have been, what you've achieved so far – and what we've got left to do.

"Let's build an extra 30 minutes into our next call/meeting so we can check in and plan how to get best value from our remaining time together."

Mid-point review – structure

Over the years I've developed an easy-to-remember four-stage structure that's been tried and tested by umpteen coaches in practice. Follow the sequence and explore each of the elements. Typically, this structure will take around 30 minutes to facilitate.

Structure for mid-point review

1. Look BACK – Review:

- Starting point/baseline, actions taken plus impacts (scaling/indicators).
- Challenges overcome/awareness gained/learning points.
- Client energy and motivation – how was the client feeling at the start?

2. Look NOW – Review:

- Where are we now in relation to baseline/goal? Are goals (and indicators) still relevant? Anything changed? Any tweaks needed?
- Are we where we thought we'd be or need to be? What's worked/helped and what's been less helpful? (May draw out drift and/or drag factors to explore).
- Client energy/motivation – how is client feeling now? (May draw out drag factors – explore as needed).
- How are we working together? Relationship/openness/trust?

3. Look FORWARD – Facilitate discussion around:

- Time/sessions left in the assignment – hours/timescales
- What still needs to be achieved? Review size of actions/steps taken – have we taken low-hanging fruit/big steps still ahead? Do we need to take bigger steps/commit to more stretching actions?
- Timeline – map out sessions/any key dates or dependencies/specific anchor points. (Creating visual timeline/working back from end (date or final session) helps to highlight time vs what's still to be done.)

4. SO WHAT? – Re-energise/reset motivation and focus on forward momentum:

- What do we need to dial up/down for remainder of the journey?
- Any changes needed to how we work? Session frequency/communication?
- Test commitment/client motivation and reaffirm your own commitment

---

Quick Tip-in-Practice: Create your own "map" for the mid-point review. Create prompt questions for each stage and make sure that you have all relevant client notes (goals, measures/indicators/actions taken) to hand.
Remember: Facilitate in adult–adult mode – and model partnership.

FAQ (this is asked more than ANY other question)...

What if we need more sessions than originally agreed?

Following a mid-point review this is a natural question; through discussion you and the client may have identified that there's still a LOT to do, and feel that the time/sessions remaining are insufficient. And this might be the case.

Equally, it's important to challenge these assumptions, and I always encourage coaches (by themselves or in supervision) to consider the following points objectively before committing to additional sessions/requesting an extension to the assignment:

Q: When we map the timeline/sessions/outstanding goals forward, what – specifically – still needs to be done? What size steps has the client taken? What steps do they still need to take? Have we left the "big" things to the end? If so, what's the MINIMUM number of sessions/time needed to achieve those "big" (often behavioural) things and embed them?

Q. Has the assignment drifted? To what extent is the requirement for additional time attributable to my management of the assignment? If a further one or two sessions are added, what will I need to do differently to stay on track and avoid further extensions?

And – really importantly – we need to hold up the ethical lens:

Q: How genuine is the "need" for additional sessions; can I sense any elements of dependency/avoidance of "the end" in the client's language or behaviour?

If – having objectively tested these points – you believe that an extension of one or two sessions would support the client's achievement of their goals, and that the client is fully motivated to focus and deliver, then you can agree/recommend this course of action.

But, like any variation to a contract, we need to approach it as a re-contracting and ensure that any original stakeholders are involved in the decision/sign-off to extend.

Quick Tip-in-Practice Re-contract for additional sessions/time; be specific and ensure it's sufficiently boundaried and recorded. Agree a maximum/end point and beware of scope creep.

E.g. "We've identified xyz as remaining priorities to work on; we have x time/sessions left in our original schedule and we've agreed/will request an additional y hours/sessions to support the achievement of your goals. We'll commit to carefully manage this additional time and we've agreed that the assignment won't extend beyond y sessions/date."

Who are the stakeholders in this assignment?
Who needs to sign off additional sessions/time/budget?
Who will make the request?

Recapping – at a glance

> **The assignment is losing momentum... what can I do?**

How do we keep up the momentum once we're underway?

- All journeys go through different phases; initial momentum may slow.
- Examine the macro assignment objectively:
  - Symptoms?
  - Test assumptions and evidence
  - Drag or drift? (Person or process?)
- Drift is relatively simple to fix. Use technology to support.
- Drag is more complex and interrelated. Explore six themes (internal/external).
- Mid-point review is a built-in scheduled review of progress and partnership.
- Four-stage structure: Typically needs 30 mins:
  - **1. Look BACK** – Review
    - Starting point – journey so far – key learning
  - **2. Look NOW** – Review
    - Where are we now? Are goals/measures still relevant?
    - What's helped/hindered progress?
  - **3. Look FORWARD** – Facilitate discussion around:
    - Time/sessions remaining – still need to achieve – actions/timeline
  - **4. SO WHAT?** – re-energise and focus forward
    - Dial up/down – changes needed – test commitment
- Craft your own mid-point "map" and prompt questions.

I believe that the mid-point review is AS CRUCIAL as the set-up and close; it's our opportunity to review the journey – from the quayside to our current coordinates – and identify what we need for the remainder of the trip. Don't forget to health-check the boat – have we picked up any barnacles along the way?

Journey's end...

Looking back on the journey – what have we **experienced** and **learned**? **Where** have we landed?

This is about **celebrating** progress and partnership, checking **what's in our kitbags** and **preparing to disembark**...

CHAPTER 10
Closing – journey's end

As I sat down to write this chapter, it struck me that the whole question of closing usually arises out of supervision. As the coach approaches the end of the assignment, they might mention "I've got one session left" and the question of closing invariably comes up.

More often than not, the coach has given little thought to the close – where it sits, what it covers, who is involved – and why it's so important.

So, the most asked question is typically:

> **What do I need to cover in the final session?**

Through exploration, this is often supplemented by questions such as:

- Is the final session the close? Do I need extra time? Who is involved?
- When do we review progress against goals and measures? Is that a separate review with the sponsor/stakeholders?
- We're closing the assignment; does that mean closing the relationship?

So before we look at what to cover in the closing session, let's briefly explore the "when", "why" and "who". Let's start with the why – the purpose of the closing session.

Purpose, role and scope of the close

My favourite explanation can be found in *The Reflecting Glass*, where authors West & Milan (2001) emphasise the importance of planning the final stage of the assignment:

> The end of a development coaching contract is a significant event.
>
> If the work has been meaningful and effective, both coach and client are likely to regard their relationship as a significant one and therefore to have strong feelings about its ending.
>
> *In many ways, the ending is a microcosm of the overall process; the more profound the learning process and relationship between coach and client has been, the more important the ending is likely to be.*
>
> There is both a business and a personal dimension to the ending process…

And it's this duality of purpose that gives closing its complexities.

You're honouring the journey undertaken together while maintaining all of the hallmarks of what made the partnership effective ("Microcosm of the overall process" – West & Milan, 2001).

> **Key outcomes to achieve – the three Rs.**
> 1. Review the road travelled – from baseline to achievement of goals/measures
> 2. Recognise the resources gained and developed during the journey
> 3. Reposition the relationship

When does the close happen? Is the final session the close?

Not necessarily. It depends on the structure of the assignment and what you agreed with the client. If you agreed: contracting + 5 coaching sessions + close then you've specifically signposted a standalone closing session.

Chemistry | Contracting + Session 1 + Session 2 + Session 3 + Session 4 + Session 5 = Close

Mid-point review

If, on the other hand, you contracted for a total number of x sessions/hours, then the client may not be aware that the last meeting will contain different elements (i.e. a review of the journey plus closing off the assignment and the partnership).

> We must honour the psychological contract with our client.
> Signpost the purpose and scope of the "last" session and allocate specific time to it.

Ideally, we'd separate the last of the coaching sessions from the closing session; but it all depends on how you contracted and the structure of the assignment.

> **Quick Tip-in-Practice:** The final session shouldn't come as a surprise; regular signposting throughout the assignment is key.
> Begin with the end in mind and use the mid-point review to signpost remaining time/sessions.
> "After today, we've got two more coaching conversations and then a final meeting to review and close off the journey..."

By signposting the final meeting as "review and closing off", you're preparing the client for a review of the assignment and an ending. This psychological signposting is key.

We've established that the closing session has a distinct role and purpose, and good practice suggests that it's separated from the last of the coaching sessions.

So, when should it happen and who is involved?

In practice the when and who are inextricably linked; there are (at least) two options:

Option 1: Review with stakeholders then close with client (one meeting in two parts)

Part 1: Review of road travelled is undertaken as a three-way review with the original sponsor/stakeholder (if you undertook three-way contracting). You'll review baseline measures vs progress indicators/observed behaviours and evaluate achievement of agreed goals and measures. (Plus, you might set some forward-looking next steps.)

Part 2: Sponsor/stakeholder leaves, you and the client examine the resources gained/developed during the journey, review and reposition the relationship.

Or

Option 2: Review and close with client then review with stakeholders (two meetings)

Meeting 1: With the client only, review journey, resources gained and reposition the relationship.

Meeting 2: Review the road travelled with original sponsors/stakeholders and invite inputs/observations. Baseline measures vs progress/achievement of agreed goals and measures. (Plus, you might set some forward-looking next steps...)

There are merits and potential downsides to both approaches:

- Option 1 gives you and the client time and space to talk through stakeholder inputs afterwards and the closing of the relationship is the final part of your interactions. The potential downside is that you'll be reviewing progress in real time, with the sponsor.

- Option 2 gives you and the client an opportunity to complete the review before involving the other stakeholder(s)/sponsor(s). The potential downside is that it may feel odd to have closed the relationship with the client and then to meet again!

Whichever option you choose, you need to take account of:

- what was agreed at contracting (**Golden rule: whoever was involved in contracting is involved in the final review.**)
- logistics/time and sessions remaining.

> There are merits to both approaches.
> Discuss the options with your client at the preceding coaching session.
> Agree the preferred option and make necessary arrangements.

Structure for the closing session

Having established that the closing elements need to be specifically addressed – and ideally positioned separately to other sessions – let's look at what we need to cover and how we might achieve this.

While every closing conversation will be different (depending on the journey, format [see options on previous page] and the relationship that's been established) it will usually (dare I say should?) contain these three perspectives, positioned here as a three-stage sequence. As always, I like to keep it super simple!

As always, I like to keep it super simple – three perspectives/Rule of 3.

Look BACK – the journey
Review journey, progress, achievements and development
Coach, client + sponsor/stakeholder(s)

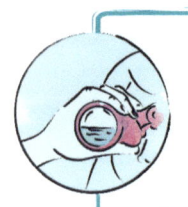

Look AROUND – horizon scanning
Short term near-future scanning – challenges and strategies
Coach, client

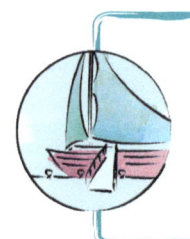

Look FORWARD – relationship and support
Relationship and support
Review & reposition – identify support/future contact
Coach, client

(These stages are explored in more detail on the following pages.)

The first stage (Look BACK) is a structured review of the journey and may involve the sponsor or other stakeholders and their inputs. The second stage (Look AROUND) and third stage (Look FORWARD) involve the coach and client only.

> **Stages 1 and 2 provide a platform for Stage 3.**
> Insufficient focus on the first two stages may result in the client feeling unprepared for the closing of the coaching partnership. Prepare for disembarkation.

Stage 1. Look BACK – the journey

This meeting – or section of the meeting (see Options on page 121) – is a facilitated review of the client's journey from the initial set-up/contracting through to the current position.

In this meeting we need to achieve the first two of the "R" outcomes:

1. **Review** the road travelled – from baseline to achievement of goals/measures

2. **Recognise** resources gained/developed during the journey

> ⚠️ Helping the client identify the tools, techniques and strategies that have been effective for them during the journey is CRUCIAL to an effective close. It builds the client's confidence in their own resources. This element is of equal importance to the review of progress/goals.

What to cover/how to cover it

This stage is pretty straightforward. You'll facilitate around a number of key themes and questions to help the client – and the sponsor(s) if they're involved in this review meeting – evaluate progress using the indicators and measures identified at the outset

---

1. Look BACK – review the road travelled, acknowledge achievement and key learning

- What was our starting point/baseline? (Refer to notes/invite inputs.)
- What actions have been taken/what are the impacts (scaling/indicators).
- Challenges overcome/awareness gained?
- Tools, techniques and strategies – what worked/didn't? Key learning?
- Where are you now in relation to what you set out to achieve (observations/inputs/feedback from sponsor/others)?
- What's still left to do/work in progress?

You're the experienced traveller, so you're leading this review. You'll ask the sponsor/stakeholders for their observations and feedback, agree the extent to which objectives have been achieved, and discuss what's still work in progress.

> 💡 **Quick Tip-in-Practice:** Maintain focus on duality of outcomes; building confidence during this stage supports the later stages of the close. Facilitate carefully to help the client to recognise their achievements through their own input or feedback from others.

The Look BACK stage might be a stand-alone meeting – with sponsor – or flow into Stages 2 and 3.

Stage 2. Look AROUND – horizon scanning

The second element of the conversation focuses on what's coming down-track; it enables the client, with the coach alongside, to:

- look ahead to the coming three to four months (don't look further ahead than this – keep it short term)
- identify potential challenges and opportunities
- develop top-level strategies to make the most of the opportunities.

> Facilitate this stage as a mini-coaching session.
> (15 mins max – keep it top-level.)
> The purpose is to help the client recognise the tools and resources they already have in their kitbag, and that they're equipped for onward travels.

By exploring future-based topics at a top level, this mini-coaching session should build confidence and resilience in the client as they recognise the range of resources and tried-and-tested strategies they already have. And they're doing it with their coach alongside them.

> **Quick Tip-in-Practice:** Apply clean, zero-content directional questioning. I.e. Use forward-based questions to explore the top-level challenges/opportunities and how they'll impact, down-based questions to check assumptions and back-based questions to develop options/strategies.

E.g. *"What are the potential impacts/consequences of xyz?" (Forward)*

"What assumptions are you making about that/what evidence might you see?" (Down)

"How similar/different is this to other situations that you've encountered?" (Down)

"What approaches have you used in the past to deal with something similar? (Back)

"How have you approached this previously?" "What's worked for you in the past?" (Back)

These clean, no-content directional-based* questions are an easy format for clients to remember – and it's generally this type of question that lodges in our sub-conscious to support self-coaching. You may notice during this mini-coaching session the client asks themselves the next anticipated question. This is a sign that self-coaching is beginning.

> It should become apparent to the client that they have more resources and confidence; they have grown and developed during the journey.
> **The client has plentiful resources for future journeys.**

*See Chapter 1 for details of no-content directional questions.

Stage 3. Look FORWARD – relationship and support

The final stage of the closing meeting specifically looks at the third of the three Rs desired outcomes: Reposition the relationship.

> Key to repositioning is what I refer to as "handing the client back into their own resources".
> As coaches, we want the client to achieve independence and to draw on their own resources using the coaching principles they've experienced with us.

The first element of this stage is to help the client identify their own resources; where/how they can access the kind of conversations that they've been having with you? This can be achieved through exploration of some key questions to identify people within their own network – and to recognise the role of self-coaching.

What to cover/how to cover it

3. Look FORWARD – relationship and support.

- Review, acknowledge and hand the client "back" into their own resources.
- Working together – what were the hallmarks of our time together? What made it different to other meetings/conversations?
- Which specific elements supported your progress?
- Where – within your own network – can you find these characteristics?
- Who/where/how can you activate that support?

Looking at the characteristics of the coaching relationship – and what made it different to other relationships – helps the client to objectively assess the relationship and its boundaries. Once they've identified the characteristics, it's usually fairly straightforward to recognise where they can find these in other relationships.

E.g. If the client recognises the hallmarks of your conversations as "dedicated time to talk about my stuff, non-judgemental and supportive" then you examine where they can find these characteristics within their existing network of contacts/colleagues.

Equally, through this exploration the client might recognise that they're already self-coaching. Initially they may notice it as your voice/approach, but this will embed further into genuine self-coaching.

"When I'm stuck, I hear you in my head", or

"I think about the question you'd be asking me and I ask it of myself."

The final line and future contact

Finally, you will need to acknowledge the journey, say your goodbyes and set out the parameters for future contact. This final close of the conversation – how we leave the relationship – will leave its own imprint.

As we said at the beginning of this chapter:

> "In many ways, the ending is a microcosm of the overall process; the more profound the learning process and relationship between coach and client has been, the more important the ending is likely to be." (West & Milan, 2001)

We will inevitably have feelings about the ending of the relationship; powerful, productive relationships take significant investment from both sides. We've invested in the journey – we've enjoyed working with the client and we're curious to know where the client travels next.

This is where our ethical coaching hat needs to be firmly in place.

> This is not about you and your needs.
> Closing this coaching partnership doesn't undermine its strength. It's the end of this professional journey and we need to close it sensitively and ethically while honouring the essence of our relationship.

We've achieved what we set out to achieve: the client has developed as a result of the work we've done together, and can recognise – and celebrate – their progress. The "task" aspect of the assignment is complete.

Now we need to ensure that the relational aspect of the partnership is acknowledged and honoured sensitively and safely.

One of our primary ethical responsibilities is to ensure that dependency doesn't develop and to be alert to potential indicators. See FAQs for more endings-related behaviour.

We need to signpost clear parameters for future contact and – of course – remind the client about the enduring nature of the confidentiality that surrounds the relationship. And, of course, remind the client about the confidentiality which surrounds your notes/conversations.

> As a general rule of thumb, confidentiality around the content of conversations/anything the client has disclosed will have enduring confidentiality, never to be shared with anyone unless required to do so (by law).

Your coaching plans/notes should be stored securely for the duration of the assignment and then routinely reviewed. Material that's no longer needed (e.g. for supervision) can be safely destroyed.

> **Quick Tip-in-Practice:** The final line(s) need to be carefully crafted to:
> - honour and recognise the relationship and the roles you've played
> - give feedback about your experience; and
> - set the tone for future contact.

There are a zillion-and-one different variations to this final close and repositioning; here's an example which uses the **Honour – Feedback – Future Contact** format.

> *"It's been a privilege to travel with you. I've really enjoyed our time together; your openness and willingness to get stuck in have enabled us to go further than we otherwise might have, so thank you for bringing that trust into play.*
>
> *"You've built on your strengths and gathered additional tools that I know you'll take forward. You're already asking yourself the questions that I'd ask you so your self-coaching muscle is already flexing."*

Tone for future contact: *"This journey's at an end, and I wish you well with your travels. If anything significant comes up in the future – and you feel that coaching could help – then you know how to access support. And maybe our paths will cross again down track."*

The words used in the future contact line(s) are crucial; if we issue an invitation to keep in touch/keep us apprised of what's happening, then we're not closing.

E.g. "Keep in touch – let me know how things are going."

This is an example of how **not** to end things. It implies that the relationship continues. This isn't an effective close and it isn't helpful to either party. Be careful of loose words. Develop your close.

> **Quick Tip-in-Practice:** Key useful words and phrases for the final line:
> **"Significant"** – " If anything significant comes up…". This signposts the scale of reasons for future contact must be "significant" and thus excludes regular updates on minutiae.
> **"Where coaching could help"** deliberately positions coaching – not YOU specifically as the coach – as a potential route to support future challenges.
> **"Maybe our paths will cross again down track"** is one of my favourite lines; it's both vague and reassuring at the same time.

The "future contact" line will be slightly different if you're working within an organisation and are likely to encounter the client in the course of your everyday. Your final line needs to focus on re-positioning and differentiating.

> *E.g. "This brings our coaching relationship to a close; as we work for the same organisation it's likely that our paths will cross when we're wearing our work hats. Rest assured that everything we've spoken about within this relationship remains confidential, and if anything significant comes up in the future where you think coaching could be helpful, you know how to access support."*

FAQs:

The client keeps cancelling the final session; what can I do?

This isn't unusual; it's one of the examples of "endings-related behaviour" that author Catherine Sandler cites in *Executive Coaching – a Psychodynamic Approach* (Sandler 2011). I can't tell you what a relief it was to find that endings-related behaviour was a recognisable phenomenon. Sandler explains: *"as human beings we seek a sense of psychological safety, defend ourselves against anxiety and are programmed to create attachments with significant figures in our lives". She maintains that some clients may seek to deny the ending – for acknowledging it is to acknowledge a loss.*

According to Sandler, examples of endings-related behaviours include:

- leaving the coach before the coach can leave them by apparently being too busy to attend the final session

- postponing the end of the coaching process by repeatedly cancelling the final session

- developing a serious new problem at the end of the programme, necessitating further work or leaving the coach feeling anxious or guilty

My experience is that the first two behaviours – related to the scheduling of a final session – are by far the most common of the endings-related behaviours.

Quick Tip-in-Practice: If gentle email prompting doesn't generate a diarised final meeting, my rule of thumb is:
Try twice then let the client know there's a "deadline" for using their remaining time. Explain how you'll allocate that time.

E.g. "Dear X, I hope you're well and making progress on xyz. I just wanted to remind you that you have one remaining session/x hours available. As discussed, this final session would usually involve a review of your journey and identification of next steps (and would typically involve inputs from x [sponsor]).

"Our usual approach is to keep this time available to you for a maximum of six months from the last meeting; we last met in (month) so I'll keep this time "in the bank" for you until (month). If we don't meet before then, I'll feed this coaching time back into the pool so that it's available for other leaders to draw on."

It's up to you what parameters you apply. I believe that putting unused time back into the organisational "bank" ensures that it's used where it's most needed. And nothing is wasted.

If your client doesn't take their final session, simply close off in writing using the "Honour – Feedback – Future Contact" format.

Recapping – at a glance

> **What do I need to cover in the final session?**

"... the more profound the learning process and relationship between coach and client has been, the more important the ending is likely to be." (Bacon & Voss, 2012)

- Define and signpost "final session". Make sure there's specific time built in for an effective close involving relevant parties (i.e. whoever was at contracting).
- Three "Rs": Review the road travelled, Resources gained, Reposition the relationship.
- Three-stage structure: Typically needs 60 mins (see Options on page 121 for different formats):
  - 1. Look BACK – review road travelled (client, coach (plus sponsor(s)):
    - Starting point – baseline – actions – impacts
    - Current position in relation to goals/indicators
    - Tools, techniques – what worked? Highlight resources gained
  - 2. Look AROUND – horizon scanning (client & coach):
    - Recognise toolkit and apply to near future
    - What's coming down track – challenges/opportunities
    - Strategies to deploy? Draw on client resources and build confidence
  - 3. Look FORWARD – relationship and support (client & coach):
    - Hallmarks of this relationship – where else can I find that?
    - Hand back into own resources (network/self-coaching)
    - Closing line(s): Honour – Feedback – Future Contact
- Endings-related behaviours: Look out for behaviours and manage accordingly.
- Dependency works both ways. Endings carry their own sense of loss; seek supervision to explore how you're feeling/plan your approach.

We've disembarked.
We've unloaded our kit and are heading our separate ways,
knowing that the relationship provided a safe vessel for this journey.

Playing in the sandpit...

We learn through **curiosity and play**.

Try out new tools – bring your favourite tools – and a bucket and spade...

Be curious.

Experiment in the safety of the sandpit.

PART 3: RESOURCES AND REFERENCES
Useful stuff

This final section offers up some additional resources, a handy cross-reference of tools and where to find them and – of course – the all-important acknowledgement of other authors and their work.

I have been inspired by many authors over the years; often it's a single phrase – or metaphor!! – that sticks with me. Having had my material "borrowed" so many times over the years, I know how important it is for individual authors – who have put massive time and effort into their work – to get the recognition they deserve.

Part 3 is split into three sections:

1. Tools and where to find them – Cross reference to the various tools mentioned in this book

2. More about – additional chapter-related resources

3. References used in this book – a list of the authors whose work I have referenced within the chapters of this book. To each of you, a heartfelt "thank you" for providing inspiration and sparking insights into my practice.

Play in your own sandpit. Be curious. Be creative.
Step back from your practice – look through fresh eyes.
What's working? What's not working?
What's the question you most want to ask?

Got a question?

If you have a specific "What if" to pose, please scan the QR code to send me your question. Whilst I can't respond individually, you may find your question answered in one of my webinars and podcasts at www.portfolio-info.co.uk/resources – or in a future article or book.

Works in progress – keep up to date at www.portfolio-info.co.uk

- Diamonds in the Sand; and
- Sand in my Shoe

ASK A QUESTION

Section 1: Tools and where to find them

Agile questions 20

Expansion questions 19

Flip or reverse questions... 19

GROW model 27

Missing questions 19

Precision questions.. 18

Rule of three 41

QAQA.. 14

TED questions 18

Three pens technique 44

Three wise mentors... 42

Tying a bow... 31

Section 2: More about
– additional chapter-related resources

In this section we will provide additional information about models in previous chapters, providing more detail.

CHAPTER 1
Hanging on a thread...

The agile* model provides four directions of questions – they don't need to be linked to content or previous questions. This is your go-to, never-leave-home-without it model.

Up – Bigger picture/Strategic
(How does x contribute/align/fit into the bigger picture)

Back – History/Experience
(What's your experience of x/How has that worked previously)

Forwards – Future/Impact & Consequences
(What's the impact of doing/not doing x)

Down – Assumptions/Evidence
(What's your basis for.../What evidence do you have...)

*Derived from Peter Hill's *Concepts of Coaching* (Hill, 2004)

Agile* questions

Up/Bigger picture

How will this contribute to...?
How does this fit into...?
Where does this feed in?
How will this affect your stakeholders?
How will this be viewed by...?
How sustainable is this in the longer term?
How is this aligned to...
How will this fit into the overall objectives?
What is the ultimate goal?
What's the context for this?
How does this compare with other...?

Forward/Consequence

How does this impact?
What would be the impact of doing/not doing...?
How would you deal with...?
What are you expecting to happen?
What's the best/worst thing that could happen?
What would be the outcome if you...
How would that affect you?
What could you do about that?
How would that make you feel?
What are the positive impacts of...?
What are the potential negative impacts of...?

Back/History

What experience have you got of...?
How have you/others dealt with...?
What has worked for you in the past?
What hasn't worked previously?
What approach have you used before?
What parallels can you draw?
Have you had problems like this before?
How did you deal with this?
What did you learn?
What helped you the most?
What hindered you?
What have you not tried that you've tried before?

Down/Assumptions

What assumptions are you making?
How do you know that to be true?
What are your grounds for believing...?
What makes you think that?
What's the basis of your belief?
What makes you say/feel/think that?
What's your evidence?
If you do... what do you think will happen?
What makes you think that?
How sure are you that this will work?
And what's the basis for your certainty?
What do others think? How do you know?

*Derived from Peter Hill's *Concepts of Coaching* (Hill, 2004)

CHAPTER 10
Journey's end – the closing

Here's a quick reference guide to the detail of the three stages of the closing meeting. Details of the "how" and potential scripting can be found in Chapter 10.

Stages of an ending conversation

1. Look BACK – Review road travelled, acknowledge achievement and key learning

- What was our starting point/baseline? (Refer to notes/invite inputs.)
- What actions have been taken/what are the impacts (scaling/indicators)?
- Challenges overcome/awareness gained?
- Tools, techniques and strategies – what worked/didn't? Key learning?
- Where are you now in relation to what you set out to achieve? (Observations/inputs/feedback from sponsor/others.)
- What's still left to do/work in progress?

2. Look AROUND – Horizon scanning – Recognise toolkit and apply to near future

- What resources do you have now that you didn't have before?
- Looking at the next 3–4 months, what challenges do you anticipate?
- Mini-coaching session using strategies/resources gained (building confidence).

3. Look FORWARD – Relationship and support – Review, acknowledge and hand the client "back" into their own resources

- Working together – what were the hallmarks of our time together? What made it different to other meetings/conversations?
- Which specific elements supported your progress?
- Where – within your own network – can you find these characteristics?
- Who/where/how can you activate that support?
- Closing relationship – safely, sensitively, acknowledging your journey.
    o Honour the relationship/thanks
    o Feedback/feelings
    o Final line and future contact

Section 3: References

To each of you, a heartfelt "thank you" for providing inspiration and sparking insights into my practice.

Chapter 1 – Hanging on a thread...

Peter Hill (2004) *Concepts of Coaching (A Guide for Managers)*. ILM

Chapter 2: Serving soggy quiche

Sir John Whitmore (2017) *Coaching for Performance*. Nicholas Brealey Publishing

Chapter 3: Slipping out of "ask" gear

Andrew Gilbert & Karen Whittleworth (2009) *The OSCAR Coaching Model*. Worth Consulting Ltd

Chapter 8: Contracting – the journey begins

Peter Hill – see above

Anne Scoular (2011) *Financial Times Guides: Business Coaching*. Prentice Hall

Terry Bacon & Laurie Voss (2012) *Adaptive Coaching*. Nicholas Brealey Publishing

Chapter 10: Closing – journey's end

Lucy West & Mike Milan (2001) *The Reflecting Glass*. St Martin's Press

Catherine Sandler (2011) *Executive Coaching: A psychodynamic approach*. McGraw Hill